Beyond Bound and Broken
A Journey of Healing and Resilience

RIA STORY

DEDICATION

This book is dedicated…

To my husband, Mack, who was God's tool to save me and later let me be God's tool to save him.

And

To my brother, who said it much better than I can:

"To have been cut through our soul is an easy excuse to quit and call our life over, but to choose to live life, to enjoy the good and face the bad with both an open mind and resolve – that is what life is."

And

To those who have been broken.

CONTENTS

A SURVIVOR'S PRAYER
By Ria Story

Thank you Lord for the gift of another day...
Help guide me to use it wisely, this I pray.
Thank you Lord for a loving husband in my life...
Help guide me to be a better wife.
Thank you Lord for the gift of health...
Help me remember the meaning of true wealth.
Thank you Lord for family and friends...
Help me be an example for good, instead of an example for the Fiend.
Thank you Lord for a chance to touch another's heart...
Help me remember that Your creation is a work of art.
Thank you Lord for the gift of free will...
Help me remember to use it for good, not ill.
Thank you Lord for forgiveness of my sin...
Help me remember it's an eternal battle we are fighting to win.
Thank you Lord for the responsibility of representing You...
Help me as I strive, when tested, to remain true.
Thank you Lord for strength in trials and tribulations...
Help me remember You temper me with those situations.
Thank you Lord for helping me forgive the one who broke trust...
Help me let go of painful memories of rape, abuse, and lust.
Thank you Lord for the stronger woman that was built...
Help me find freedom from a false sense of guilt.
Thank you Lord for helping me heal from corruption and abomination...
Help me remember it's a journey, not a destination.
Thank you Lord for bringing me to a safe place...
Help me let go of the shame, and claim grace.
Thank you Lord for the gift of Your Son...
Help me remember the battles that through Him, I have won.

You can download a copy of this prayer on my website: www.riastory.com

DEAR READER

God doesn't cause the pain in our lives, but He uses it. Whatever you have gone through in the past or are going through now, never forget I love you, God loves you, and He has a special purpose and plan for you.

If my words touch your heart, then pay it forward. Give a copy of this book to someone else. The world needs more hope.

I would love to hear how this book changed your life. E-mail me at: ria@riastory.com

I am praying for you!

RIA STORY

PROLOGUE

I am proud to be a survivor because that means I survived.

Regardless of the past, or the present, we have the ability to survive and even thrive. Healing from the wounds life deals you isn't easy. For some, the scars will fade with time. For others, the scars will always be there and will forever remind you of the wound.

Scar tissue isn't pretty, but it doesn't hurt any longer.

Healing is a journey, and we have to take it one step at a time. One day at a time. One hour at a time. One minute at a time. Maybe, even one breath at a time.

Beyond Bound and Broken is "the rest of the story," sharing the lessons I learned about how to start to heal and how to truly live life. Some of you may prefer a chronological account of my story. If so, you can find that in *Ria's Story From Ashes To Beauty*, available online at Amazon.com and RiaStory.com.

After *Ria's Story* was published, I felt like I was finished writing for a long time, perhaps forever. But, less than six months later, I realized there is so much more to be said about learning to live life "after." I had no idea just how many others would share with me a similar story of brokenness, abuse, or of being a victim. I had no idea how many would share how they found encouragement, hope, healing, and inspiration in my story. I also had no idea so many who were not victims of abuse but had experienced something painful, terrible, or traumatic would find encouragement, hope, healing, and inspiration in my story.

I don't pretend to have all the answers. *Ria's Story* was a first attempt at baring my soul, but even a year later, I realize how much I left out because I simply didn't have the strength to be vulnerable. At 110 pages, it was all I could do to write that much, and I had nothing left to say beyond those pages. I didn't have the courage to show you all my scars.

Perhaps I still don't, but I have a new confidence in my God-given purpose, and "*I can do all things through Christ who strengthens me.*" (Philippians 4:13) I am not a counselor, a psychiatrist, a doctor of anything, or a therapist. My claim to expertise is having lived what you will read on these pages, and then, making it my life's work to share with others how to be resilient.

Is there fear? Yes. Anytime we are vulnerable, there is fear. When we are open and transparent, when we expose our soft side, when we open our heart and soul, we always do so with some level of fear. Fear that being truly honest about whom and what we are will cause others to reject us. Fear that some people can't, or won't, accept our honesty. Fear that if we tell the world we aren't perfect, we won't be loved.

Is there shame? Yes. I struggle even today with a sense of shame, and perhaps, I always will. One of my biggest challenges is releasing that to God's grace and accepting His love.

Is there doubt? Yes. I know there is a temptation to question or doubt God and His plan – I've done it myself. Sometimes it felt like God was so far away. I questioned if He even really existed. But, through it all, God was there, and He has redeemed me. He has used the pain in my life to temper me and prepare me for a purpose. I am now beyond bound and broken.

The worst years of my life become a good thing when I realize I can use them for good. I can use them to bring hope to someone else. I am fulfilling my purpose when I help someone else realize, that no matter how bad life gets, we always get to choose how we respond.

I won't pretend my story is the worst thing that could have happened to me. Certainly, it left me scarred in many ways. It also shaped me, defined me, and then, refined me.

It breaks my heart to know so many others have suffered as I did or even worse.

My heart breaks for those who have suffered in other ways, like the mother who has lost a child to cancer. My heart breaks for the husband who lost his wife in a car wreck and must raise their three children as a single father. My heart breaks for the young boy who is bullied in school until he takes his own life.

I don't know what plan God has for bringing you through the darkness to the light, but I do know He has a plan. I do know God has brought healing to me, and He can, and will, bring healing to you. You only have to accept it.

Some wounds in life heal quickly and easily, but others scar the soul forever. Any kind of trauma – emotional or physical trauma, physical or sexual abuse, losing a loved one, losing a job, losing a limb, losing yourself, just a few examples I could name – can leave us with scars from the wounds. Sometimes the scars are physical, visible and tangible; sometimes the scars are emotional, mental, and psychological.

Sometimes, the bad times can be forgotten, as can the good. Often, there are memories you can't walk away from and can't forget. It doesn't matter how big or how deep they go. Healing doesn't mean there was never a wound there. Healing means the wound has closed over, and there is no festering infection. While there is a scar, it will fade with time. What matters is how we heal from the damage. We have to learn to be resilient, to rebound, and spring back. Lou Holtz said, *"Life is 10% what happens to you and 90% how you respond to it."*

I realize more each day how incredibly blessed I am to be traveling this life journey with my husband Mack. Without him, I wouldn't be the person I am today. He is, and has always been, incredibly supportive of me, encouraging me to find my way forward.

It can't be easy, being the spouse of an abuse victim. Actually, it's probably not easy to be a spouse at all! But, being the spouse, parent, or even the child of an abuse victim brings a few more challenges.

There are times I simply need space, room to breathe, time to think, and a little extra grace in our relationship. Too often, I don't share what I'm thinking or feeling because it feels safer. These are the times I am so fragile that to touch me would shatter me. The only way I know how to protect myself is to pull back into my shell.

For years, even after we were married, I wasn't secure in our relationship because I wasn't secure in myself. I thought sharing my pain or my struggles would drive him away. I thought no one could love me broken, so I pretended to be whole. How beautiful it is now to realize I don't have to pretend to be perfect. I don't believe in "soul mates" because I believe God is my soul's companion, but I do believe my life's companion should, and will, love and accept me for who I am. Sometimes, my steps forward are only inches, and yet, I need him to applaud each one as though it were a giant leap. And, he does. I wouldn't be the woman I am today without him.

I'm a survivor, and I learned how to survive. I would have gone on surviving, somehow, someway, even if God had not sent me a knight in a shiny Camaro. But, would I have learned to thrive?

I believe God places people in our lives. Sometimes,

it's for them to help us. Sometimes, it's for us to help them. Maybe, it's both. We all touch the lives of the people around us, even though we don't always know it.

I pray that through my words I touch your life for the better. I pray that I touch everyone for the better. Ralph Waldo Emerson said, "*To know that even one life has breathed easier because you have lived. This is to know that you have succeeded.*"

"How did you do it?" is a question I get asked often. As in, "How did you manage to move on and live life after years of being abused sexually and emotionally?" My first attempts at blogging and writing tried to answer that until I realized I really didn't have a pat and perfect answer.

I don't believe in a miracle cure or a one-size-fits-all plan to move from surviving to thriving in three or twelve steps. We all have a different path to walk on our journey, and we must walk it, just like everyone else, one step at a time. I can only share my journey with you and pray you find inspiration and courage for your own.

Your pain may be different from mine. Your journey almost certainly has been. Or, perhaps it's not your journey. Perhaps you are a spouse, loved one, parent or friend who needs to read a true, no holds barred account of some of the things your loved one is going through or has been through, an account of the things he/she wants and needs to say but can't. Everything they wish you knew but can't tell you.

Like any daunting task, sharing my journey with you and writing this book seems overwhelming, and at times, much bigger than I am. There are some days it would be so much easier to go back to a regular job with a steady paycheck that doesn't require me to be *more*. A job that doesn't require me to be strong yet vulnerable.

I refuse to turn back, because I'm in the HOPE (Helping Others through Positive Encouragement) business. I won't give up on the thousands and thousands of people out there who need hope to start the healing journey, to break free of their own bonds, and to live life beyond broken, one day at a time. I refuse to turn back because a life lived in the shadows of the past is a life not fully lived. I know because I've been there.

Beyond Bound and Broken

Chapter One
THE RESILIENCE FACTOR

"The greatest glory in living lies not in never falling, but in rising every time we fall."

Nelson Mandela

I learned far too young that life isn't fair. Raised on an isolated farm in Alabama, I was sexually abused by my father from age 12 – 19. I was dressed up, photographed nude, beaten, tied up, raped, emotionally blackmailed, and psychologically abused. I was forced to play the role of a wife and even shared with other men due to my father's perversions. Desperate to escape, I left home at 19 without a job, a car, or even a high school diploma.

I don't think there is "complete healing" here on earth. God gives restoration, but we don't ever forget or completely get over the effects of our brokenness because it shapes who we are. But, you can find the place of resilience.

I wasn't always resilient. I don't think you can learn to be resilient until you have lived through the dark and have come through to the light.

Resilience. Just the word makes you want to sit up a little taller or lift your head a little higher. Resilience is the ability to recover, to spring back, to thrive, and to become strong after, or in spite of, weakness. Resilience in others inspires us, and we admire those who have learned to thrive. Resilience looks glorious when we see it in others because we only see the triumph, not the struggle. We only see the light after the darkness, and in truth, that's all we want to see. It's only inspirational when we see the worthwhile fight and the victory.

Some people master resiliency at an early age, while others may not find it until old age. Some never find it. Some people learn to be resilient to some circumstances, but not others.

The journey of resilience can be broken down into three phases. These are emotional stages, not physical ones.

The first phase is the most difficult. It's the dark time when you are actively living through despair. I call this the Captivity phase.

The second phase is the Coping phase where you are out of the worst of the situation, and you are "okay" but still bound and broken inside in some places.

The third phase is the Conquest phase where you have overcome and can now call yourself resilient.

How fast and how quickly we rise to resilience is determined by our Resilience Factor, our ability to move beyond surviving to thriving. The higher our Resilience Factor, the greater our ability to overcome whatever happens to us in life and move from the Captivity phase to the Conquest phase.

Captivity

Captivity can come in many forms. We can be in Captivity to emotions and feelings like fear, anger, doubt, shame, or guilt. We can be in Captivity to food, drugs, drama, alcohol, gambling, sex, work, exercise, bad relationships, or any addiction. It's not as much what we do as why we are doing it that determines if we are in

Captivity to something. Captivity can be an overindulgence or a starvation, when either one is done for the wrong reasons or to our detriment. Sometimes we are in Captivity to a need to control ourselves or others, or we are captive to other people and what they say or think about us.

Because this is emotional Captivity, it may or may not show outwardly, at least at first. Sooner or later, it will show up. In the words of Robert Morris, *"A physical bruise is caused by inward bleeding. A person's skin is hit, and at first there is no outward sign...Emotional bruising can follow the same course. A person suffers through rejection or loss or hurt, and at first there's no outward sign. But inwardly the person is bleeding, and soon the signs of that hurt will appear for anyone to see."*

The Captivity phase for me lasted until I was physically able to leave my parents' home at age 19. I left behind years of hopelessness, physical restriction, sexual abuse, and emotional despair.

Growing up, on the surface, things seemed okay. Maybe not normal – anyone could, and did, see my dad was too "familiar" with me. I dressed in clothes he bought me that were too tight, too revealing, too sexy. I barely spoke to anyone. I didn't date or even talk about boys. I wasn't allowed to socialize much, and we were isolated from church, school, and family.

How often we turn a blind eye to the things we don't really want to see. Or, we are willing to see but don't know what to look for. Or, we see what is going on but don't want to "get involved in something that's not my business."

I was desperate for help but didn't know how to ask for it. So, I didn't allow myself to think about it because to do so meant coming perilously close to the edge, and I was afraid I would fall off.

Satan attacks the hardest when we are down, not when we are strong.

I didn't realize I could emotionally overcome my circumstances without physically leaving. I was emotionally living in captivity because it was the only way I knew how to survive. The only way I could protect "me" was to build a strong wall to shut out the chaos of the outside world. So, I did.

In this phase, we may even refuse to acknowledge there is a problem.

Coping

In the Coping phase, we are still struggling with some issues inside. We aren't in complete Captivity any longer, but we are still fighting a battle internally over something. We have moved beyond complete despair, but still have wounds inside.

We have acknowledged there is a problem and taken some steps to overcome. This is the "rebound" phase, or the healing phase, where we have hit the bottom and are on the way back up. This phase could last for minutes or years, and there are some people who will never find the next phase. We each travel a different path, and there isn't a wrong way or a right way, just your way, which is different than my way.

After leaving my parent's home and the Captivity phase, I stayed in the Coping phase for thirteen years. In fact, I stayed until I realized I was the only one holding myself back.

The Coping phase can be deceptive because it's easy to tell yourself you have overcome whatever battle you were fighting. Dissociation is a survival mechanism, protecting us from the force of whatever happened. But, the event or trauma itself hasn't truly been processed, only stored. The lie I told myself was that I had left my past behind, and it wasn't affecting me, which of course wasn't true.

I didn't want to define myself as a victim. I didn't want others to define me that way. I still don't. I told myself I was perfectly fine – I didn't have anything to heal from. It was many years before I purchased even the first "self-help" book for abuse victims. I started reading it and never finished it. "I don't need that stuff." I told myself. It was only after I had written my own book that it occurred to me to look again for resources to aid my healing. When I did start reading some of those resources, I realized I wasn't the only one to have felt those feelings of rejection, shame, and worthlessness.

Our past always affects us. We don't get to leave it behind like it never happened. That would be like losing a leg and going around trying to pretend you could still function exactly the same. You can lose a leg and learn to walk again, but it will be different. Emotional healing is very much the same.

From 2000 to 2013, I was Coping, and Coping pretty well, but I still carried some of the burdens I had brought from Captivity around with me. Shame, guilt, depression, and a feeling of unworthiness were always tucked away in a little corner ready to come out again if I let them. Anytime I was feeling especially vulnerable about something else that wasn't going quite right in life, at work or at home, those feelings would start whispering to me, compounding whatever else I was dealing with.

Ultimately, it's our decisions and determination that will allow us to leave this phase and move to the next, but until we reach the Conquest phase, we are much more vulnerable to influences that hurt us.

Be careful who and what you allow to influence you, especially in areas where you are still not strong. It's important to be mindful of what thoughts you allow yourself to think, what words you allow yourself to say, and what actions you allow yourself to take.

Even a little tiny crack can grow to destroy a strong foundation if we let it. Be very careful to seek the positive things you want to grow in your life, instead of the negative things you want to leave behind.

Conquest

The third phase is the Conquest phase when you are truly living in the light and have reached a complete victory over the past, or even present. Let me be clear – you can physically be in a prison, but emotionally you are able to reach this phase, and you are in a place of light

This phase is only possible with God's love, healing, and forgiveness and isn't dependent on anything except you.

I couldn't have written this book five years ago because I hadn't achieved victory at that time. I had learned to be resilient in many ways, but I was still on the rebound emotionally about my past.

Conquest is just that – complete victory. When we are living Beyond Bound and Broken, we are living in this phase. We have mastered resilience and have learned to thrive in spite of our circumstances. That doesn't mean life gets easy all of a sudden – far from it. It simply means we are better equipped to deal with the storms of life because we have learned to be resilient. The more resilience you have, the faster you can spring back up when life, or Satan, knocks you down. There will still be times when you get knocked down, but now you have learned how to get up again and again. This is the place where you have learned to find contentment in the small things as much as the big things.

I reached this phase on August 14, 2013 when I told a room full of 200 people I wasn't going to let my past hold me back, and in doing so, I proved it.

The greatest step for me on my rise to resilience was realizing I didn't need anyone to empower me. God had already empowered me. When we talk about empowering someone, we really mean equipping them, giving him or her tools or knowledge to help them. Resilience comes from within.

Emotional resilience isn't dependent on your physical circumstances.

We always have the freedom to choose resilience. Viktor Frankl, concentration camp survivor, said, "*The last of human freedoms is the ability to choose one's attitude in a given set of circumstances.*"

We always have the freedom to choose faith over fear. We always have the choice to claim grace and have gratitude. Someone close to me once said, "*Freedom is such a sacred thing that not even God Himself imposes His will on any man.*"

To be resilient, I had to learn to change my thoughts. There is no reason to spend energy in wishful thinking, fantasizing that my parents had been the parents I wish they had been. I had to accept reality and move on.

It's so very simple and yet so difficult to do. To move through each phase and ultimately reach our own victory, we must start by changing our thoughts. Our thoughts will determine our feelings, and our feelings start to determine what we do, what we say, and where we end up.

To change my thoughts, I had to change the way I was thinking and what I was thinking. I started to do this by reading books and listening to audios that were focused on thinking positive and how positivity can affect you overall.

Norman Vincent Peale said, *"Our emotional life is profoundly regulated by our thought life."*

It's not that I was a negative person, even when I was in the Captivity or Coping phase. Far from it, I've always known on some level keeping a positive outlook and attitude was the only way to be effective in living life and overcoming negativity. I have always tried to identify what I have to be thankful for, rather than reacting to what I have to be bitter about.

It's not that I've ever let myself stay negative for long, but when I became more intentional about positive thoughts, attitude, and intentional personal growth, I rapidly accelerated myself to the Conquest phase. Once you discover a new way of thinking, you can't go back and un-think it!

You've heard it before – "Garbage In, Garbage Out." When I learned to start changing my thoughts on purpose by focusing on controlling them, rather than letting them control me, I rapidly realized which thoughts didn't serve me well.

It's much like realizing you can affect your health by putting good food into your body instead of junk food. If you put good materials into your mind, you can affect your emotional health in much the same way.

I probably take it farther than some people. For example, I'm not very tolerant of Facebook "friends" who post negative words, pictures, or comments. If someone posts something negative, I simply "un-friend" them. I don't mean someone sharing their struggles, I mean someone sharing something rude, crude, ugly, profane, demeaning or anything along the lines of blaming someone or putting someone else down. I unfriended someone just today for tagging me in a political post without my permission.

Another example is how I don't spend time with negative people. I've left behind friends in the past, not because I'm better than they are – I'm simply focused on a positive direction. If we aren't going to the same place, there isn't any reason to travel together.

I don't want negative emotions even getting a tiny foothold in my life. That's a door I don't want to open.

I know it sounds simple. It is simple. But, simple doesn't mean easy. It's something I've learned to do over the years, and I've learned to do it much better in recent years. I expect I will continue to improve as I develop my mental discipline in this area. I don't expect to be perfect at it, but I will always be trying to get better.

The only person who can change your circumstances is you. God helps us in many ways, but many of those ways are the abilities, intellect and capabilities He gifted each of us with. He expects us to use them.

RIA STORY

Questions for Contemplation or Group Discussion

1. In what areas of your life are you in the Captivity phase? The Coping phase? The Conquest phase?

2. What are some ways you can focus on more positive influences in your life? (Some examples could be friends, social media, books, songs, etc.)

3. Think of one or two ways you can intentionally say, or do, something positive this week.

4. Read, reflect and/or discuss these bible verses: Romans 8:31; Romans 8:38-39; Lamentations 3:22-23; 2 Corinthians 4:16-18

Chapter Two
FINDING FORGIVENESS

"To forgive is to set a prisoner free and discover that the prisoner was you."

Lewis B. Smedes

Forgiving Yourself

According to some statistics, 1 out of 6 women and 1 out of 33 men in America have or will be the victim of sexual assault in their lifetime. And, those are just the reported statistics. I would imagine there are many others who never report what happened to them. Sadly, what happened to me isn't that rare.

The secret I carried around with me was ugly. It was dirty. It was festering inside. I was too ashamed to tell anyone – my dad started sexually abusing me when I was 12 years old. I was innocent. He was not. He would wait until we were at home alone, and then, he would make me dress up for him, so he could take pictures of me. He would tell me it wasn't a sin because God had given me to him to fulfill his needs as a man since my mother didn't. He told me no one else would understand.

It progressed, as I got older. By the time I was 17, he was regularly sleeping with me and would bargain with me for sexual favors in return for something like an outing with my friends. He started sharing me with other men, whom he would connect with on the Internet, so he could help me find an "ultimate experience in life."

An ultimate experience meant lots of things. One time it meant taking nude pictures of me riding my horse. One time, it meant tying me up naked and beating me with a riding crop until I was black and blue. One time, it meant watching while another man had sex with me. And then, they changed places.

Concentration camp survivor Viktor Frankl was a psychiatrist who shared his experiences and insights from imprisonment in his book, *"Man's Search For Meaning."* It's a profound story because of the depth of suffering he, and so many others, tragically experienced along with his realization that regardless of our circumstances, we have the ability to choose our response and attitude.

What struck me when I read this book was the realization that each of those survivors almost certainly had to learn to forgive his or her self. Frankl shares: *"On the average, only those prisoners who could keep alive who, after years of trekking camp to camp, had lost all scruples in their fight for existence; they were prepared to use every means, honest and otherwise, even brutal force, theft and betrayal of their friends, in order to save themselves. We who have come back, by the aid of many lucky chances or miracles – whatever one may choose to call them – we know: the best of us did not survive."*

I can't imagine the depth of his experience or how he learned to survive and later forgive himself for doing so. But, I know an important part of my ability to move forward to healing was finding a way to forgive myself for my actions. It doesn't mean I would do things differently in life. It does mean I realize I can't change the past, and I can't have peace if I can't have forgiveness.

By age 17, I was living a life of sin and deception. Driven desperately to escape, I sought any outlet I could find. When I discovered the Internet, it was only a matter of time before that became a source of corruption. I started meeting with people whom I had met online, sneaking out at night to do so, and then sneaking back inside before morning. No easy task, since I had to climb out of my bedroom window, climb down off the porch roof to the ground, and then walk three quarters of a mile just to reach the county dirt road.

It became easier and easier to slip further away from the pure heart I had once had. By that point, I was playing the role of a surrogate wife every night for my dad, including intercourse, and I didn't see any reason not to become sexually involved with someone whom I had met online, someone I thought might "rescue me."

It didn't last of course. This happened a few times - he would get what he wanted and move on, and I would once again be searching for a savior in the next man I would meet. When one wanted to take nude pictures and even a video of me, I didn't say no. It was several months later when I realized why he pushed me so hard to participate in the video and pretend to be enjoying it. He was selling pornography on the Internet. He had been involved in trafficking and selling pornography for minors, including me, and the FBI tracked me down through him.

I reached a new low point when they contacted my parents and told them. The agents asked me to testify against the man, but I refused to say absolutely anything at all or even talk to them. They wanted to talk to me in private, but dad made it clear on the drive down to meet them he would be present for any and all interviews. I knew better than to go against him. The agents didn't realize, of course, that my dad's anger wasn't the shocked feelings of a parent who realizes his daughter is sexually active, but the jealous and possessive nature of a man who felt like his "wife" cheated on him. I kept my sunglasses on and wouldn't even look at them.

I was more than ashamed, I felt violated, betrayed, and guilty. I harbored unreasonable anger toward everyone – the agents for contacting my parents and destroying my life, the man for violating my privacy so completely, and my dad for punishing me for what I did. He sat me down in front of my mother and brother and told them what I had done. Then, he demanded to know when I had my next period, so they would know I wasn't pregnant.

I found the whole experience humiliating. He was having sex with me. He knew I was on birth control because he bought it. He also took me to a clinic and made me get tested for HIV/AIDS and punished me for "endangering his life" by having sex with someone else. He would righteously lecture me, and then, go right on with his relationship with me.

There is so much from that time of my life I would rather just forget completely. I don't think saying I'm ashamed of my actions really conveys the depth of pain, guilt, and worthlessness I felt. I felt like I was such a sinful person, and no one could love me for me instead of for my body.

I still find it difficult to talk about and admit the things I was doing. I would give quite a lot to be able to go back and change it. But, I realize I must forgive myself.

We can't change the past however, and regardless of what bad decisions we have made, we have to move on and forgive ourselves. For me, that only happens when I realize God has offered me forgiveness. It doesn't mean I will ever stop regretting some choices I made, but I won't continue to beat myself up for it. Forgiveness of self comes before forgiveness of others.

Forgiving Others

Soon after publishing my book, *Ria's Story From Ashes To Beauty*, I had a local book signing in my community. I was sitting at a table with a sign about my book, and of course, there were books for sale if someone wanted to purchase one. One man walked up and stopped briefly to read the sign before approaching the table.

"I just have one question for you," he asked me, "Is he dead or in jail now? He deserves one or the other, and I know you won't rest until he gets it."

Shocked, I mumbled something about it wasn't important at this point. I always think of great responses after the fact. But typically, I verbally stumble around when I'm surprised by a question or comment. The man moved on, leaving me with my thoughts.

His question assumed I still held hate in my heart towards my dad, and I don't. I certainly wouldn't wish harm on someone because I was wronged.

When we can't offer forgiveness, it only poisons us. Forgiving someone does more for us than it does for them. If we continue to hold on to anger or hurt or resentment, we will be unable to find peace. The other person may not even realize it, and it only hurts us if we hold on to a wrong done. Even worse, sometimes we feel like we have a right to retribution when someone hurts us.

No one has a right to do wrong, regardless of whether someone has wronged him or her. You've heard the saying "Two wrongs don't make a right." How sad it is when two people get divorced, and one person feeling wronged, seeks to make the other one pay for it, usually at the expense of the children they had together.

I talked about forgiveness in *"Ria's Story From Ashes*

To Beauty" from the perspective of how much it helps us when we forgive someone. That's a large part of my message - how we can choose to forgive. Sharing my message to help others is why I shared my story to begin with. It's not about seeking to hurt someone else because I was wronged – it's about letting go and moving on. I received a message from a reader, and as always, I'm humbled when my words help someone in their own journey:

"Ria I just finished reading your book.... I will admit I had been hesitant to read it because of the things I knew from your past life.

I think you handled things beautifully and showing how you have forgiven so many people and moved beyond the horrible things that happened in your childhood... So what I got out of it was that there are things that have happened to me in the past year that I need to forgive and forget and move beyond and refocus my life back on promising positive things.

The most important part of the book is the paragraph, which says forgiving another person is part of our own personal growth journey. We must choose to move forward down the path rather than backwards. If there is something in your life you need to forgive, or if there is something you need to let go of in order to move on, and of course the answer is yes, and so that's what I will be working on."

None of us are perfect, certainly not me. There are times when, even inadvertently, we will hurt someone else, and we need forgiveness just as much as others do. The Bible says, *"For if you forgive men their trespasses, your heavenly Father will also forgive you. But if you do not forgive men their trespasses, neither will your Father forgive your trespasses."* (Matthew 6:14)

The more someone loves you, the more power you have to hurt them, and the more forgiveness you will need from them when you do hurt them.

The more you love someone else, the more power they have to hurt you, and the more forgiveness you will need to extend them when they do hurt you.

Forgiveness is a gift you give yourself. The other person might not even know or care if you forgive them, but the difference it makes in your life is everything. Forgiveness doesn't mean forgetting. It does mean letting go of the blame and the bitterness. Holding on to those negative feelings will only hurt you.

One more thing on forgiving someone else – you shouldn't approach them and tell them you forgive them, unless they ask. Forgiving someone has everything to do with your feelings toward them and not their feelings toward you.

Martin Luther King, Jr. said, *"Darkness cannot drive out darkness; only light can do that. Hate cannot drive out hate; only love can do that."*

Forgiving God

Where was God when I was suffering? Where was God when my dad told me his only regret was "not starting sooner" so he could have watched my breasts develop? Where was God when I hated my dad for taking away my privacy? Where was God when I found myself so ashamed of what dad was doing with me that I begged him not to tell my mother? Where was God when I was being raped while my father watched and then took his turn? Where was God when I was tied up and beaten with a riding crop until I was black and blue? Where was

God when my body betrayed me, and brought me shame, by responding when I didn't want it to? Where was God when I cried out in despair and wanted to simply give up living?

We need to forgive ourselves. We need to forgive others. And, we need to forgive God. Not for His sake, but for ours. In the words of Mahatma Gandhi, *"The weak can never forgive. Forgiveness is the attribute of the strong."*

Playing the victim role allows us to hold on to anger and blame someone or something else for what happened to us. Norman Vincent Peale said, *"Many people suffer poor health not because of what they eat but from what is eating them. If you are harboring any ill will or resentment or grudges, cast them out. Get rid of them without delay. They do not hurt anybody else. They do no harm to the person against whom you hold these feelings, but every day and every night of your life they are eating at you."*

Sometimes, we suffer consequences from the decisions of someone else. Sometimes, we suffer from the consequences of our own mistakes and decisions. Sometimes, terrible things happen, even to those who don't deserve it.

I love the story of Job in the Bible. Whenever I start feeling sorry for myself, I remember Job and how he suffered because Satan wanted to test him. Job lost almost everything. He lost his home, his children, and his lands. He suffered from boils all over his entire body. His friends, and even his wife, told him to curse God. But, he would not. Job knew God is the source for good, and not evil. Job questioned God, but then he repented, and God restored him in the end.

It's natural to have doubts or to want to question God. We are human, and we all make mistakes. Remember though, the bigger the battle, the greater the victory when we overcome.

God doesn't cause the pain in our lives. God didn't cause my dad to do what he did, or my mom to stand by him. God gives us the freedom to choose for ourselves. Satan tempts us to make the wrong choices. We live on earth with pain, suffering, and sin. Bad things will happen to good people. I had to learn to let go of my anger and stop blaming God for my situation. I had to learn sometimes we pray for a miracle, and the answer is no.

Today, I still pray for miracles, but I also pray for peace with God's answer.

Questions for Contemplation or Group Discussion

1. What do you need to forgive yourself for?

2. What has God given you forgiveness for?

3. Is there something in your life you need to ask someone else to forgive?

4. Who do you need to forgive?

5. Read, reflect and/or discuss these bible verses: Matthew 6:14; Acts 3:19; Ephesians 1:7; Psalms 103:12; Romans 12:2

Chapter Three
DECISION POINTS

"Today I choose life. Every morning when I wake up I can choose joy, happiness, negativity, pain... To feel the freedom that comes from being able to continue to make mistakes and choices - today I choose to feel life, not to deny my humanity but embrace it."

Kevyn Aucoin

"Are there days you forget?"

I was standing outside a conference room checking my email on my phone. It had already been a long morning preparing and setting up for the conference Mack and I were hosting, and it wasn't even lunchtime yet. I looked up at the man who asked me the question. He had been in the conference room when my book trailer, *Ria's Story*, was played a few minutes earlier and had walked outside to find me. He had to walk outside to find me because I couldn't sit inside while it was being played. I didn't want to stand there, watch it with hundreds of other people, and feel like they felt sorry for me when they learned "my story."

Even today, I fight the feeling of dread when it comes time to hand someone a bookmark that tells even the barest details about my story and me. I cringe inside whenever I'm standing there, and someone mentions my story. There is something in the pit of my stomach that curls into a little ball when Mack references my past to someone, even though he does it in a wonderful and supportive way. It's nothing to do with him – it's me. On an intellectual level, I realize it's silly. I wrote the book so I could talk about it, share my experiences, and help others. But, I don't really want anyone to know about my past.

So, I couldn't stay in the conference room and watch while my book trailer was playing. All those people in there, most of whom I knew, would now know the truth about me.

"Are there days you forget?" He waited for me to respond.

Decent manners demanded I answer the man, even if he was simply asking from curiosity. I took a deep breath to answer him, but he continued talking. "The reason I ask is.... I was abused too. It wasn't my father. It was my grandfather, and I was real little, about 8 years old when it started. He kept doing that to me until I was 13." The man looked away from me and struggled to maintain composure. "I didn't tell anyone for a long time. But since my grandfather died, I've talked about it now with my wife some and my sister. I just wondered if you ever forget because there isn't a day that goes by that I don't think about it. I'm hoping it gets better."

My heart broke for him, and I instantly regretted my thought that he was simply asking from morbid curiosity. I couldn't imagine what he was going through. Years and years had passed since he was abused, but he clearly lived it over and over again every day.

The answer for me is "No, I never forget." For many years, I wanted to forget. I pretended to have put it all behind me like it never happened. I refused to talk about it and dodged around any questions about my parents. But, I'll never forget. I don't think we can forget experiences in life that shape who we are today because they are so much a part of who we are and why we are what we are. It would be like asking a Holocaust survivor if they ever forget.

For me, it's not about forgetting the past. It's about learning to live life again in spite of the past. It's about learning to take those steps forward in life and leave the past behind. You may never forget – but the victory comes in learning to live again. Make the decision to move on. Sooner or later in your healing you will face a decision – move forward and live again or stay forever stuck in the pain of the past.

There are many experiences in life I treasure and remember with a smile. There are many experiences I certainly DON'T treasure, and I hope I never have to experience anything like them again. I bet we've all had both extremes when it comes to experiencing what life has to offer.

The good times – Mack getting baptized, our wedding day, our 14th-anniversary-14-mile-hike, my stepson Eric sending me a text message on Mother's day, and so many more – are certainly far more pleasant to remember than the hard times.

The hard times – leaving my parents' home because I was running away from being sexually abused for years by my dad, holding the hand of my dear sweet Granny and singing Amazing Grace to her while she passed away, moving away from our home in Auburn – are the times we sometimes don't want to remember.

Those times, although difficult, are often times of growth. But so often, I find I don't truly appreciate that until after it's over.

Growth is a good thing. It means becoming more of who God intended us to be. However, it's rarely easy and usually requires giving up something. The problem with that is we feel the loss so much quicker than we realize the gains. And, none of us really WANT to give up something. In the words of the famous cliché, we want our cake, and we want to eat it too (Who doesn't?).

Even so, we know to go up, we must give up. And on our good days, we do. Sometimes life happens, and we don't have a choice. But more often, it's a decision point we face, and we can choose to move forward or turn around. We don't like it, we may cry over it, and knowing it's going to be to benefit us in some way seldom softens the blow. But, on an intellectual level, we understand that is the cost. So, we do it.

I thought about this while running a marathon recently. I started out that morning with the goal of completing my fourth marathon and hopefully completing it in less than four hours, which would be a personal record. I put the work in to train and prepare. I ate well. I practiced. I did long runs and short runs. I did everything I could to set myself up for success. Almost.

It was overcast that day, but the temperature was already hot. With over 90% humidity, I simply couldn't keep my body cool. I ran right on my target pace for the first nine miles, but I had been drenched with sweat since the second mile. My visor was so wet the Velcro wouldn't stick, and it kept slipping off my head. I finally took one of the safety pins from my bib and pinned it through my visor, while running, so I could keep it on.

My shoes were SQUISHING with every step. At the nine-mile marker, I suddenly had a cramp. I walked through it, and then, picked back up my pace. I was a few hundred yards back from the pace group, still plenty of time to recover and catch up. But, by mile 10, I had to concede I couldn't keep up. I walked through the next water station and took two cups of water, trying somehow to stay hydrated. I knew I needed another gel, but I was already feeling sick from the heat and just couldn't make myself take one.

At mile 11, I tanked. I hit "the wall" far sooner than I should have and much sooner than I ever had in the past. Right about then, I came up on the split where the full marathon runners keep left and the half-marathon runners turn right and run the two miles back to the finish line.

For the first time in my life, I seriously considered quitting. I knew since I was already hurting and cramping the next 15 miles weren't going to be pretty. I knew I could simply turn right and be done in less than 20 minutes. I could come up with any number of excuses to justify quitting. I knew if I kept running, the next few hours would be more mental than physical, and it would certainly be a growth experience as I developed that "mind muscle" of self-discipline.

I was already dehydrated. There was no way I would be able to take in enough water to rehydrate like I should. I clearly wasn't going to make my goal of a personal record, so why keep trying to finish? What's the point? I didn't want to spend the next three hours thinking about whether I should have trained harder, rested more, run more, started sooner, eaten more, or eaten less.

I thought about how it was going to be tough to keep going, how hot it was already, and how much I simply wanted to sit down and rest. I thought about it.

Then, I thought about what the rest of my day would be like if I quit. I thought about the drive home, the rest of the weekend, the rest of my life, and telling everyone who had supported me I simply gave up because it wasn't going to be fun or easy. I thought about the T-shirt I wouldn't wear with pride and the medal I wouldn't hang up because I didn't earn it. I thought about giving up on myself because it was easier to quit than to keep going. But, I kept going.

It wasn't pretty. I hurt. My muscles cramped up. I very nearly cried several times. But, running was hard enough, and I didn't have the extra energy for tears. I texted Mack and told him I was going to finish even if I had to walk the rest of the way. I knew I was in trouble when the other runners started asking me if I was okay…and the medic on the golf cart started following me. I kept going – and when one of the other runners simply lay down on a bench and stopped, I said, "Not me." and kept going.

I watched runners pass me who were thirty years older and wished them well. But, I kept going.

I think the medal I earned that day is my favorite because I worked harder for it than any other. It's not about the medal or the T-shirt; it's what they represent.

It's knowing I didn't quit, although I wanted to, more than I wanted anything in a long time. It's knowing when I face a decision point, in a marathon or in life, I know I will make the right decision, even though it's not the easy decision. Because nothing worth having comes easy, or cheap. And, if it's worth starting, it's worth finishing.

We all face decision points in life, much like I faced at that mile marker. Turn around? Or, keep going?

Consider all the decision points you face each and every day. There are many opportunities to make choices in life. Each day, we make hundreds, if not thousands, of choices. What to do, what to eat, where to work, who to talk to, or what to watch on TV. Whether we wake each day with a positive attitude or a negative attitude is a choice. Whether we snap at the kids or gently remind them to hurry and get ready for school is a choice. Whether we are hurried and rushed every day because we take on too much and fill every minute with something is a choice. Whether we have good or bad daily habits is a choice.

The choices we make each day, either consciously or not, affect the rest of our lives.

I hope you have already made the choice to start healing and start changing your life for the better. I hope that's why you are reading this book. It's not a question of if we will have to overcome something in life – it's just a question of when and what. And, how bad it will be.

Questions for Contemplation or Group Discussion

1. What life decision(s) are you facing today?

2. Is there an area of your life that is out of balance?

3. What daily habits do you have that are serving you well (prayer time, exercise, etc.)?

4. What habits do you have that are not serving you well? (Saying "yes" to everything, not getting enough sleep, etc.)?

5. Read, reflect and/or discuss these bible verses: Matthew 7:13-14; Proverbs 16:9; 1 Corinthians 10:13

Chapter Four
THE FIRST FEW STEPS

"We are products of our past, but we don't have to be prisoners of it."

Rick Warren

Jaycee Dugard is a good example of someone who has learned to take life back after being broken. If you don't remember, or aren't familiar with her story, Jaycee was abducted when she was 11 and held captive for 18 years. She was used, abused, and somehow survived. She had two children, fathered by her abductor and rapist, and they too were held prisoner. I can't imagine what she went through.

Actually, I can. I can imagine and relate, perhaps too well, to some of her feelings and emotions. I find myself compelled to read the stories of other "victims," and yet, it's always difficult for me to do so. On one hand, I want to learn how others have coped with similar circumstances as what I endured, and on the other, I don't want to know what they went through because it brings back so much of the past for me.

My story isn't her story, but there are certainly a lot of similarities. Jaycee says, "*I don't think of myself as a victim. I simply survived an intolerable situation.*" I wish I could give her a huge hug and let her know I understand. I understand her desire to be heard, her fear of sharing her story, and her difficulty in writing about what she went through. I understand why she became a prisoner in her mind, as well as physically. I understand why she was unable to leave, in the later years of her captivity, even though she had access to the Internet and even some outings where she could have escaped.

Jaycee's book is titled "*A Stolen Life.*" I understand that too. She lost 18 years of her life, and she won't ever get those back. Life doesn't come with an "Undo" button. Rightfully so, she feels like those years were stolen from her. I feel much the same about my own years as a teenager. Those should have been happy years of developing self, discovering purpose, and developing my passion. Instead, those years have many memories I wish I could forget.

I wish I could give Jaycee a hug and tell her I'm proud of her choices and decisions since August 26, 2009 when she took her name and her life back. I'm proud of her and her decisions to create something good from her years of loss, pain, and hardship. I'm proud of her for facing her fears and being strong enough to be vulnerable. I'm proud of her because she is determined not to let the rest of her life be stolen too. It's not easy to take life back. The first few steps are often the hardest.

Here are some ways I started taking those first few steps on the road to hope and healing.

Decide To Be Grateful

I love birthdays. Not just my birthday (although I admit it's one of my favorites) but also everyone's birthday. I love the idea of celebrating someone on his or her special day. Like any holiday, my birthday comes with a touch of sadness for me because my parents should be celebrating with me but they aren't.

After I left home, a part of me really and truly expected my father would ask for forgiveness for years of abusing me, and I expected my mother to support my decision to leave such a toxic environment. I thought they would want me to be happy, and clearly, staying in a situation where my father was sexually abusing me was not healthy. A small part of me actually believed they would come around.

But, they didn't. I talked to my father for the last time, only a few weeks after leaving home. He called because it was my birthday. But to my complete shock, he told me I was going to suffer eternal damnation for leaving home, and I needed to return to him. I just hung up the phone, devastated and crying too hard to talk any more.

Right then, I faced a decision point. I could carry the bitterness and pain with me for the rest of my life, souring everything else from that day on. Or, I could let it go. I made a commitment to always have an attitude of gratitude. In the words of Denis Waitley, *"Happiness cannot be traveled to, owned, earned, worn or consumed. Happiness is the spiritual experience of living every minute with love, grace, and gratitude."*

The Serenity Prayer is familiar to most of us. Attributed to Reinhold Niebuhr, the verses resonate with truth: *"God grant me the serenity to accept the things I cannot change; courage to change the things I can; and wisdom to know the difference..."*

Serenity to accept the things I cannot change...to me, that means accepting the things in life I cannot change with grace, peace, and understanding that God uses all things to work together for our good (Romans 8:28).

Courage to change the things I can change.... to me, which means having courage to change my attitude when it needs it. Courage to give up what's comfortable and follow where God leads me. Courage to help someone, even when, especially when, it comes at a cost for me.

Wisdom to know the difference...to me, that means knowing what I can and should change and knowing what I need to let go of. Charles Spurgeon said, "*Wisdom is the right use of knowledge.*"

Oprah Winfrey tells us, "*What you focus on expands.*" That's another way of saying our thoughts control our feelings and our feelings control our actions. I could spend the rest of my life focusing on the pain of the past. That would expand into bitterness or even hate. Or, I could spend the rest of my life focusing on what I am grateful for. Gratitude and attitude is a choice. Serenity is a choice. Courage is a choice. Wisdom is making the right choice.

Decide To Serve Someone Else

October and November of 2000 was a tough time in my life. Leaving my parents' home had turned everything in my world upside down. On top of the anxiety about leaving home and an abusive father, I was also dealing with the rejection from my mother. I was fighting off the sense of shame and guilt that more than seven years of sexual abuse had given me, and I was learning to live in a world where everything was new. New city, new home, new relationship, and a new me.

Realizing I needed a job, I took the first one I could find – waiting tables at a pizza restaurant. I was determined to make some money fast and start supporting myself. One of the perks of working the day shift was the pizza buffet. After the buffet hours were over, we threw any uneaten pizza slices away. We were allowed to take it home if we wanted. If you got lucky, there would be almost a whole pizza left!

I met "Mary" (*The name of this individual has been changed.*) within a few days of starting my new job. She was hired at the same time I was, also as a waitress. She usually worked the shift following mine. One day, she called in sick. She said she had some trouble and wouldn't be able to work that day. When she showed up the following day for her shift, she had a terrible bruise on her cheek and a black eye. I soon noticed a pattern – every few weeks Mary would suffer an "accident." Sometimes, she begged me to cover her shift on the tables. She would stay in the back washing dishes, so she wouldn't have to be seen. To make matters worse, her car broke down. Then, she didn't have a way to get to work. Often, I would pick her up and take her to work if our shifts lined up. I knew she needed the money badly – her little boy was about four years old. She was trying to save up, so she could afford to move out of the trailer she was living in with the man who hit her.

One day, some customers came in just a few minutes before the buffet ended. We had to cook several pizzas, so they would have a selection to choose from.

There was almost a whole pepperoni pizza and about half of a supreme pizza left over when I closed down the buffet line. I'm not sure what made me think about it, but I knew Mary wasn't scheduled to work for a few days. I knew she often depended on the leftover pizza. Rather than boxing up the pizza for later to take home, I asked permission to clock out for my break. I had to act fast – my break was only 15 minutes.

I quickly loaded up the pizzas in my car and drove to Mary's home. She opened the door in amazement, and her little boy came hurtling out of the door. He almost knocked me down when he grabbed my legs and hugged me; he was so excited to see the pizza boxes in my hand!

Right then, it didn't matter that my father had done horrible things to me. It didn't matter that my mom stood by him and blamed me for it. It didn't matter that I felt ashamed of my past and wanted to forget it all. It didn't matter because I realized the incredible gift of being able to help someone else. It wasn't a big act – it didn't even cost me anything, only a little time on my break. But, when we serve someone else, we get far more than they do. Sometimes, helping someone else gives us a reason to go on.

Mack and I were privileged to serve on a team of John Maxwell Team Coaches in 2013, teaching leadership to the leaders in Guatemala. We volunteered to go and paid all of our expenses. We wanted to give, and we wanted to serve. But, we felt like we received so much more than we gave. It was truly a life changing experience. Every time I speak, someone shares with me how I've impacted his or her life. I love getting messages and emails from someone who has read my book and wants to share how I have positively lifted them up and made a difference for them. When we are able to help someone else, we find the true meaning of life.

Rabbi Harold Kushner said, *"Our souls are hungry for meaning, for the sense that we have figured out how to live so that our lives matter, so that the world will be at least a little bit different for our having passed through it."*

Regardless of your situation and how difficult it might be right now, when you are able to serve someone else, add value to someone else, and lift someone else up, you will find yourself making the world better – and that gives your life meaning. Take a step toward a life that matters – help someone else. It doesn't have to be big or expensive.

Just be conscious of ways you can brighten someone's day.

I saw a Facebook post one morning from a former co-worker. She was asking friends to send a birthday card to her brother who suffers a mental disability. Like all of us, he LOVES to receive personal mail because it shows someone cares about him. It took just a few minutes of my morning to send a card. So little, and yet, so big at the same time. We underestimate the impact we can have in the lives of the people around us.

Decide To Make Good Memories

One late summer afternoon, I received a heartbreaking phone call from a lady who needed some advice. She had just learned a close member of her family had been a victim of abuse by another family member. She was devastated. Their family relationships were shattered and she wasn't sure what she should do. I don't like to give advice. Too often, well-meant advice is given without access to all the facts of the situation. I much prefer to listen intently, ask questions, and help the person find their solution to their situation. However, I was glad to be able to give her some resources for her and her family member. One of the things I shared with her was the importance of making good memories with her family as they move forward.

A question other abuse victims frequently ask me is "How do I start the healing process?" We are all different, and yet, we have all lived with the pain of past experiences.

Whether you are learning to live again after being sexually or physically abused, losing a child or spouse, or suffering a life-shattering physical injury, I believe one critical step to beginning life "After" is to start living. I don't mean merely existing. I mean truly living. Getting started can be the most difficult part. Perhaps, you don't feel like you deserve to live, laugh, and love again. Perhaps, you just don't feel like going on because it takes too much effort. Perhaps, you have lost hope and can't yet see the beauty in life "after."

Starting to heal means truly living again. One of the best ways to do that is to just start LIVING. Be intentional about planning good experiences to create good memories. It doesn't mean you will forget the bad ones – they will likely always be a part of you – but it does mean starting the process of rebuilding life by giving yourself something positive to look forward to, and then, something positive to look back on.

I'm very intentional about spending time making good memories with friends and loved ones. I plan ahead, sometimes months and months in advance, so I have something to look forward to and something fun to look back on.

In 2009, I was on a business trip in New York when one of my friends called me. She heard about an adventure race and asked me to partner with her, telling me it involved some running, biking, and a "little" kayaking. I agreed, thinking it sounded fun. I didn't find out until the night before the race it also involved crawling through a mud pit, jumping off an old lock into the river, rappelling down an 80-foot rock face, navigating through the woods with a compass, and various other challenges.

I thought that first race would never end. We argued over who was paddling the wrong way (both of us), who would be the one to rappel (I lost), and who got us into this mess (she did). More than five hours after the start, we dragged one another over the finish line, soggy, muddy, exhausted, blistered, sunburned, still friends, and very happy.

We both have birthdays in October, and it's become our tradition to celebrate each year by racing. Since that first race, I think we've only missed once because I was traveling. Its one way I very intentionally spend time with her creating good memories together.

Mack and I also focus on creating memories. Rather than giving each other gifts, we create a memory together on special occasions. One year for our anniversary, we hiked Stone Mountain, not just up it and down again but also all the way around the bottom of it! One year, we spent the entire Thanksgiving weekend in a chalet with my extended family. One Christmas eve, I had to work until after 6:00pm, so Mack went out and bought ingredients for a special dinner we cooked together.

Wherever you are, whatever you are going through or recovering from, make some plans today to create good memories with friends and family. It doesn't have to be elaborate, but do something fun together – volunteer for a service project, plan a 5k together, spend the whole day outside at your local park with no cell phones, or maybe skip the gym one morning and sleep in with your spouse. Don't wait until you feel like it. Don't wait for the "perfect time" because now is the perfect time. Make good memories and take steps along the road to healing.

Questions for Contemplation or Group Discussion

1. What are you grateful for today? Spend 5-10 minutes writing down your gratitude list. Be as specific as possible.

2. What opportunities do you have this week to serve someone else and add value to him or her?

3. How can you do something intentional each day this week for someone else? When? Where? Who?

4. What is one good memory from the past to reflect on?

5. What good memories can you plan, right now, to look forward to? Think of opportunities to spend time with loved ones, fellowship with friends, and family.

6. Read, reflect and/or discuss these bible verses: Ephesians 1:16; Colossians 3:17; Galatians 5:13; Matthew 23:11

Chapter Five
FACING FEAR

"Our deepest fear is not that we are inadequate. Our deepest fear is that we are powerful beyond measure. It is our light not our darkness that most frightens us. We ask ourselves, who am I to be brilliant, gorgeous, talented and fabulous? Actually, who are you not to be?

You are a child of God. Your playing small doesn't serve the world. There's nothing enlightened about shrinking so that other people won't feel insecure around you. We were born to make manifest the glory of God that is within us.

It's not just in some of us; it's in everyone. And as we let our own light shine, we unconsciously give other people permission to do the same.

As we are liberated from our own fear; our presence automatically liberates others."

Marianne Williamson

Marianne Williamson's words touch me because they resonate with truth. We are born children of God, created in His image, and gifted with talents and ability to be an example of His glory.

And yet, somewhere along the way, most of us forget or lose sight of that. Often, life is difficult, and we lose sight of our truth, what we were created to be, as we battle through the daily struggles. I know that was true for me. My situation before leaving my parent's home was so dark I lost my sense of self-worth. I considered throwing away what God gave me, even to the point of throwing away my life.

I'm not proud of that. I felt such a burden of fear – fear that I would never be happy or have peace. Fear that I would always be hiding – living life like nothing was wrong and yet dying a little more inside each day.

Sometimes, when you lose hope, you simply want to give up. It would have been all too easy to simply give up then, and I thought about it. I always felt like I was dragging around a huge sack with all my problems stuffed in it.

I started to deny my pain. I thought if I refused to admit there was pain, there wouldn't be any. It wasn't true, of course. Pretending something didn't happen to me or didn't hurt wouldn't make it go away; it just made me start building a wall up around my heart. Brick by brick, I started building a hard shell, so no one could ever reach me. Telling myself I was tough, I succeeded only in lying to myself.

I ran away from home several times, but the most memorable one happened just a few days before Christmas. I don't even remember what started it. Dad was mad about something I did or didn't do and kept me, and probably everyone else in the house, up all night long as he lectured me about how I needed to repent from my sin.

The following morning, I decided to leave home. I was 18 and legally old enough – it was a "simple" matter of getting out. I packed a bag with as much as I could stuff in it. Then, I got a trash bag for some more stuff. Clothes, shoes, and a few keepsakes were important to me. I got my dog, Solomon, on his leash and told my dad I was leaving, and he couldn't stop me. I think he didn't believe I would actually go through with it. First, he just told me to leave because I didn't belong in his house anyway. I started down the hall from my room, as he followed, lecturing me about my need to repent from the devil's ways.

By the time I reached the stairs, he was furious and started yelling and throwing things down the hall, and then at me, as I dragged my bags and the dog down the stairs. The CD player came crashing down on me when I reached the bottom and headed for the door. Crying by this time, I just put my head down and kept going. Carrying far too much, I started dragging the bags behind me, determined not to leave behind any of my things. I almost panicked when the dog tried to run off. I knew he wouldn't be safe if my dad found him. I tied the leash to my wrist, so I could use both my hands.

With a sense of relief, I took a last look at the house before I rounded the curve of the driveway, certain I wasn't going back. It was almost two miles of walking down the driveway and the dirt road to a neighbor's house where I could finally knock on the door and ask to call my grandfather to come get me.

I stayed with my grandparents for a day or so, refusing to return home even at the pleading of both of my parents. I wouldn't tell anyone what was wrong; I just said I wasn't going back. I knew if I started telling the truth the whole situation would turn ugly, and all I really wanted was to find some peace. I didn't want my dad to go to jail, which was what he always told me would happen if I ever told anyone what he did to me. He also told me he would go to hell if I ever decided I didn't want what he was doing to me. Since "I wanted it," God wouldn't condemn him for it.

I guess he was afraid I would tell someone. Two days after I left, he started having chest pain and had to go to the hospital. I remember my mom calling to tell me if I ever wanted to see my dad again this might be my last chance. I was already burdened with shame, guilt, and unhappiness. I knew I couldn't bear it if my dad died because of my actions. It was somehow "all my fault."

I finally agreed to go to the hospital and see him. When I got there, I remember a social worker wanted to talk to me separately, but she couldn't get me alone. Dad would know if I told someone, so I wouldn't even make eye contact with the lady. I tried to pretend everything was fine, normal, and I could go back home and be the good little daughter again, which I did.

I thought I was never going to escape. I had fought so

hard that time to get away, but I ended right back where I started. I couldn't see any hope for things to change. Ever. I wasn't allowed to date, work, or go to college. I was stuck in a web of deceit where I was emotionally blackmailed into playing wife for my father. He told me my mother wasn't fulfilling wifely obligations, so it was my job to fill in. In addition to that, I was sneaking around, meeting people on the Internet; desperate to find a savior and believing the true Savior who offered me redemption had simply forgotten me.

I was also afraid, deep down inside, that I deserved what I was going through. Dad would preach to me for hours on end, using religion to keep me in line with what he wanted. He would tell me how my heart wasn't in the right place and Satan was telling me lies to get me away from what God wanted. Then, he would turn right around and use me, telling me the whole time what we had was special, and secret, and God had provided me as a blessing to him.

I was afraid too, that no one would ever want me if they knew who I really was or the things I had done. I was afraid if I told someone the truth about what was really going on when dad "tucked me in" at night I would be the reason for my family breaking up. I was afraid if dad had another heart attack it would be my fault again, and he might not live through the next one.

I lived in constant tension – trying to keep the peace in our family by taking on all our burdens as though they were my fault. Fear can hold us back but only if we let it. So often, whatever we are afraid of is so much bigger, harder, or worse when we think about it. We can talk ourselves into, or out of, just about anything. I'm not talking about a healthy fear, like the fear of poisonous snakes, I'm talking about an unhealthy fear, where we let fear hold us back from where we need to go or what we need to do. Here are some of the fears we all face from time to time.

Fear of the Unknown

Nelson Mandela said, "*I learned that courage was not the absence of fear, but the triumph over it. The brave man is not he who does not feel afraid, but he who conquers that fear.*" Every year, when my friend and I participate in our annual birthday adventure race, there is always a challenge that involves jumping off of something. Two years ago, it was a huge rock about 20 feet above the river. I was terrified of slipping and falling or hitting the rock if I didn't jump far enough out. I didn't want to jump. I finally made myself jump, but I didn't get a good push off of the rock and ended up landing almost face down right in the water. I hit so hard my life jacket came apart, and it knocked the breath out of me.

Fortunately, I was not hurt, but I hated that part of the race. So much so, that I dreaded the next year because I didn't want to jump off of that rock again. I kept hoping maybe they would change it up and take that part out. No luck – it was back the following year.

We climbed up to the top of the rock. It was wet and steep. We had to run down to the rock edge and jump off. I knew I didn't want to do it because it was such a terrifying experience the year before. I was truly scared of getting hurt. My friend jumped. I got right to the edge twice before I backed up again and let some others jump ahead of me. I knew I would jump, but I knew it would take me a minute to overcome my fear.

We really only have to overcome fear for just a few

seconds. Once we get started, and it's too late to turn back, we aren't afraid any longer. Facing my fear of jumping was a good thing. I jumped and wasn't hurt. Even though it wasn't fun, it wasn't nearly as bad as I had imagined.

It's okay to have fear. Sometimes, it's even healthy. We should respect fear if it's healthy, but not let it overcome us. For example, I have a healthy fear of being in a car wreck, so I buckle my seat belt every time I get in the car. But, I don't stay home all the time and avoid driving because of the fear of being in a car wreck.

Our fear of failing can hold us back. If we are too afraid of making a mistake in life, we won't attempt to do anything. And, if we don't attempt it, we certainly won't be successful. Identify fears and face them if they are holding you back - and then work to overcome.

Fear of Change

We often fear change itself. As a rule, we like things to stay constant in life. Comfortable. Consistent. We don't like unpleasant surprises, and some of us don't like surprises at all. We work hard through college, so we can be comfortable in a good, stable job. Most of us find that major change is most uncomfortable.

Even when I was desperate to leave home at 19, I was terrified of what changes that would cause. What would I have to do? Where would I go? Where would I live? How would I survive? What if I didn't have any money? What if no one would believe me? My world would change drastically. That scared me. But, we can't let the fear of change hold us back. Viktor Frankl, Holocaust survivor said it well, *"When we are no longer able to change a situation -*

54

we are challenged to change ourselves."

Don't be afraid of change. Embrace it, accept it, and maybe even look for it! If nothing changes, nothing improves.

Mack and I moved away from Auburn this past summer, which meant a lot of change. Some little changes, like learning where to grocery shop in a new city, and some major changes, like leaving our home of 12 years behind. Nothing stands still in life though, and sooner or later, we will all experience change. The sooner we learn to embrace it and become comfortable being uncomfortable, the sooner we can overcome the fear of change.

I recently read an article by Joyce Meyer. The article was titled "Life Beyond Abuse." Although I didn't write it, I could have. There are so many similarities in what Ms. Meyer experienced and what I experienced growing up.

What caught my eye in the article was her definition of Abuse: *"Abuse is defined as 'to be misused, used improperly or to be wasted; to use in such a way as to cause harm or damage; to be treated cruelly.' Any time we are misused or used for a purpose other than what God intended, it's damaging."*

That last sentence is what struck me as powerful: *"Any time we are misused or used for a purpose other than what God intended, it's damaging."*

I have experienced that. As she goes on to say, God uses those difficult times in our life for our own good. It's not that period of my life I want to focus on however. I want to focus on the "life beyond" part. There was a time in my life when I was being used for a purpose other than what God intended, but there has also been in my life a time when I wasn't using my life for a purpose in accordance with what God intended.

There was a time in my life where I felt God leading me to share my testimony. I did what every steadfast, faithful, trusting, grounded Christian does when God reveals a purpose for our lives – I ran as fast as I could in the opposite direction! Okay, maybe that's not what everyone else does. At least, it didn't take a whale to change my mind.

During that six-month period in 2013 where I refused to follow God's plan for my life, my life wasn't being used for God's purpose. I was misusing the resources God gifted to me. I was afraid of the changes doing so would cause in my life.

I'm in alignment now, and I have peace about that. I've met so many people who don't have peace in their lives. Perhaps, they too have felt a "nudge" to be using their time, talent, and energy for a specific purpose, yet find themselves facing the fear of making changes. Maybe, they are facing the fear of leaving people behind in their life as they grow and follow the path God wants them on. Maybe, they fear stepping out in faith.

Perhaps, it's the fear some of us hold deep inside, that we aren't "good enough" for what God plans. I know that was my biggest fear for a long time, and to some degree, I still struggle with that. I've come to realize though, God doesn't need us to be perfect. In fact, He only uses imperfect people because there isn't any other kind!

He equips us, and then, He calls us. He wouldn't call us if we weren't ready or able. What we must decide is, are we willing?

Fear of Failure

We will certainly make mistakes in life and experience what some people consider failures. It's only a failure if we don't keep trying. If you tried it once and it didn't work, don't let fear hold you back.

I shared earlier some of the details of my second attempt to leave the home of my parents. Most people would consider it a failure – after all, I ended up right back where I started, minus my portable CD player which broke into a thousand pieces when Dad threw it at me and hit the wall instead. I admit, I didn't even consider trying again for a while. In fact, I didn't try again until Mack came along to give me a strong arm to lean on.

I'm sure I would have tried again eventually, even without his support. I started saving a little bit of money after that failed attempt just before Christmas. My parents didn't have credit cards and maybe not even a bank account as far as I know. I'm sure they had credit cards at some point – creditors were always calling the house wanting money – when our phone worked that is.

They mostly just used cash, and I started saving a few dollars any time I could without my dad catching me. It might be just a dollar or two I kept back after being sent to buy groceries, but I was building up something for when I finally found the courage to leave again. It wasn't a fortune, but I was willing to walk out with less than a few hundred dollars to my name when I finally did leave.

I met Mack in June of 2000. I was supposed to be going bowling with a friend but instead went to Auburn to a nightclub. I changed clothes on the way and then again on the way home, so my parents wouldn't know what I had really been doing.

It didn't take long before Mack started suspecting

something was strange about my situation. He made me show him my driver's license to make sure I was really over 18 because I wouldn't let him call my house or meet my family.

I was just glad to have a license to show him – I didn't get one until I was 19, just a few months before I met him, because my parents didn't believe in having driver's licenses. They finally allowed my brother and me to get one – mainly due to a new state seat belt law where you could be stopped and checked for not wearing a seatbelt. They also didn't believe in paying taxes, having insurance, and they believed social security numbers were the "mark of the beast."

I didn't have a high school diploma because I had been schooled at home my entire life, except attending a private kindergarten at four years old. The vehicle I drove was an old Rodeo that was registered to my mother and wasn't even really mine. I had never had a job or ever been to school. I was not well equipped to join society as a productive, successful member.

When I decided I was leaving my parents' home, and I wasn't going back, I asked a friend to go back with me to help me pack. I was afraid I needed support to face my parents and tell them I was leaving.

Angels were with us. We somehow drove up to the house without the dogs barking and walked boldly in the back door and upstairs to my room without being seen. We packed most of my clothes and my meager stash of savings. We surely weren't quiet, but no one noticed us. We left again without confrontation, a complete blessing, as I am still not sure I could have faced him. I remember turning around on the way out and seeing my dad sitting in the living room, facing away from us, but he never turned around and never saw us.

Mack offered me a place to stay or offered to take me to my grandparents. I chose to stay at his house, knowing that being at my grandparent's house hadn't worked out in the past. It was too easy for my dad to come get me there. Even in light of the fact I had already tried to leave twice and failed, I was determined to learn from the past and try again. I wasn't going to quit even though I was scared to death. I finally had someone on my side who guessed the truth and offered me a haven. He loved me in spite of the fact that I carried a burden of guilt and shame. He cared about me even if it meant I didn't stay with him in the long run.

Not long after leaving my parents' home, I wrote myself a letter. I was struggling with the fact that my parents were still trying to get me to return home, even two or three weeks after I had left. In the letter to myself, I mentioned I finally had found some peace and had come to terms with not going back. I also talked about how I wished Mack were a Christian (He was not saved at that time, nor was he for the first 12 years of our marriage), and I wished I could share the joy of the Lord with him.

I questioned whether I was facing the end or a beginning. Now, I see the answer was both. An end to a lot of pain, struggle, hardship, doubt, fear, deceit, temptation, guilt, and loss but also a beginning to a new chapter of love, life, laughter, hope, faith, redemption, freedom, and God's perfect healing.

That doesn't mean I don't still face fear or struggle at times. It means, I don't quit trying because there is fear or failure. It means, I face my fears and failures each day, and know even if I'm not successful, I can keep trying.

Questions for Contemplation or Group Discussion

1. What fears do you have right now about the future and the unknown? Are they healthy fears or unhealthy fears?

2. What happens to us if we are afraid of change or afraid of making mistakes?

3. Think about when a child learns to walk. What happens when the child falls down again and again? What lessons can we learn from that?

4. Read, reflect and/or discuss these bible verses: Psalm 34:4; Philippians 4:6-7; Luke 12:22-26; Proverbs 3:5-8

Chapter Six
DEALING WITH DOUBT

"God specifically planted you where you are for his Divine purposes."

Mina Nevisa

The few first weeks after leaving home were a blur for me. There were a few attempts by my parents to get me to come home again. I finally shared with my mom why I wasn't going to come home. I felt certain she would agree with me that I shouldn't return and probably she wouldn't either.

But, that's not how it worked. First, she told me I was making it up to be spiteful. Then, she told me I was mentally ill, and she was going to talk to a psychiatrist about me and had done so in the past because I was so deceitful. I made her leave and cried in despair when she did. I only saw her one other time when she came to my job at the pizza place, and told me in spite of what my father had done, I should return home for "complete healing" since it was really my fault he had done all of those things to me.

By that point, I was weary of dealing with them and being told I was going to hell for my actions.

I didn't have health insurance. I tried a few different places in the Auburn area to find any resources available for abuse victims but only found one mental health counseling resource that offered a reduced rate. I really didn't feel like I needed counseling. Everyone else felt like

I did, so I went. It wasn't productive, and I ended the sessions within two months. I never really considered there might be other resources available to me. Ironically, it was when I decided to write *Ria's Story* that I discovered there were other resources.

Please note – I'm not saying therapy or counseling is a bad thing, and I'm not suggesting you shouldn't take advantage of it. I will say the right counselor or therapist is important, and each person must decide for himself or herself the right option.

There are a wealth of resources out there if you need therapy, and I encourage you to consider them as needed. There are support groups, books, therapists, prayer or church groups, counselors, and mental health professionals. Friends, loved ones, and family members often are willing to help as well.

So there I was, working a waitressing job, making $2.13 an hour, living away from home for the first time, away from family and friends, and engaged to marry a non-Christian man with three previous divorces. Statistics would tell you it was a relationship doomed to fail. I was certain in my heart God had brought me to that place and had given me more than my share of miracles. When doubt reared its ugly head, I ignored it. For the first time in my adult life, I had found some peace.

So often, we doubt God and His plan for us because we are quick to let doubt take over when we can't see the future clearly. Often, we know what the right decisions are, but we second-guess our intuition and our inner spiritual guidance. It doesn't help when the right decisions are not the easy decisions.

Often, as survivors, we doubt we are worthy of love, or success, or having happiness ever again.

I read a beautiful book, *"Finishing Well My Daughter's*

Journey Home" written by my friend Janice Pitchford. Janice shares the story of her daughter Dawn, her battle against terminal illness, and how she faced adversity with grace and faith. The story is beautiful and heart wrenching at the same time. As I read, what I noticed most was the tremendous love and fierce protection Janice and her husband had for their daughter.

I was surprised to find myself a little emotional, wishing my parents had demonstrated that level of protection and example of faith for me. I simply cannot understand how a father could not only fail to protect his daughter but be the instrument for harm done to her.

How could things become so twisted and wrong for a father to even consider incest with his daughter? Even as I wrote *Ria's Story* last year, I continued to look for an answer, a reason, a WHY. Why me? Why such pain? Why did I have to go through years of emotional and sexual abuse? Why do I have to carry those memories for the rest of my life? Why couldn't I have a "normal" family? What was so horribly wrong with me that my mother either didn't see or didn't care that I was being abused? Why didn't she save me?

Most of us learn early, life isn't fair. Some of us learn it better or earlier than others, but we all face it sooner or later. There will be, or may already have been, times in your life when you are facing pain, illness, loss, and the search for your own answer to "WHY?"

Years and years after leaving home, I was sitting in a conference room in Orlando. I heard Les Brown say, "You have a story and someone needs to hear your story." I thought at the time if anyone had a story, I certainly did.
But, I didn't want to share it. I felt God's hand guiding me to talk about my story, I knew it would help someone,

but I doubted. I doubted I could do it. I doubted that was God's purpose for me, and I doubted God knew what was best for me. Six months later, I was given an opportunity to speak on stage. Again, I felt God's gentle nudge to share my story. I stepped out in faith and shared a piece of me and my story that I hadn't talked about for thirteen years.

Faith changes your life when you believe – but you have to believe first. In spite of my doubts, God was telling me He would help me, guide me, and prepare me for what He had in mind. And, I still didn't want to do it. I swallowed my doubts and trusted God would give me the strength for what He had in mind. It was the right decision but certainly not the easy decision.

The temptation might be there to question God and why He allows pain and suffering. In those times, I remember the words of Jesus, predicting his own death: *"Now My soul is troubled, and what shall I say? 'Father, save Me from this hour'? But for this purpose I came to this hour."* (John 12:27) When we doubt, it's because we can't see the whole picture. That's why faith is required, because we don't know for certain. It's only when looking back that we can see the whole picture. When we step out in faith, we trust there is a purpose, a plan, and a reason; we just don't always know it. Stop letting doubt talk you out of life.

Focus on Action

We've got to first decide what it is we need to do, and then, decide to do it. Often, our inner voice, intuition, or the Spirit, guides us with a push. But, so often, we make excuses about why we shouldn't do something or why we can't do something. When I knew I needed to share my story, I thought of a hundred reasons why I shouldn't do it. I told myself I couldn't do it without crying, so I shouldn't try and risk making a fool of myself. I told myself it might cause hard feelings from my grandparents. I told myself it might force me to face my parents at some point, and I really didn't want to stir up the past. I told myself people would treat me differently if they knew the truth about me.

Sometimes, when we face doubt, it's doubt in our own ability to implement a course of action. For several years, I've wanted to break four hours in a marathon. One year, I came within nine minutes. I know it's a possible goal. Something that might prevent me from making the decision to try again is doubt in my ability to follow through on training. There is something that whispers I wouldn't succeed, or maybe, I'm just not fast enough, so I should not try again.

Sometimes, when we face doubt, it's because we don't want to commit to the work required to change. I often see this in the gym when I teach classes where a participant will come up to me after class and talk about how they want to make a change like losing weight. Many people will talk about it, and then, talk themselves out of it by making excuses – "I'm too busy with work to eat healthy right now" or "I don't have time to exercise regularly" or "I tried to get healthy for New Years last year, but since I didn't stick with it before, I know I won't stick with it again so why bother" or one of my least favorites, "My husband won't eat healthy, so it would be too much work for me to eat healthy."

Making the decision is only the first step. We must stop wishing for something to change and start taking action. Even when we have doubts, once we are committed to something, it only becomes more difficult the longer we wait to do it.

After I spoke on stage in August of 2013, the next natural step was to consider writing a book about my story. Everyone suggested that would be a great resource for others who experienced similar situations to mine, and I agreed. I decided to do it, and that's where it ended. I started a few times, typing up a few pages on my laptop. I quickly realized deciding to do something is only the first step. Actually carrying out the decision is much harder. I didn't like remembering the time from my life where I was in despair and out of hope. I didn't want to bring back memories of pain and fear. I wasn't ready to share the part of me I had kept hidden for so long. I doubted whether I was ready or whether I was equipped to write such a book, and so, I kept pushing it away.

It's not enough to wish for something. Even in the face of doubt, we must take action if we want to overcome those doubts. Start small if you need to. For me, it was writing just a little bit for a speech. Then, I worked my way up to a whole chapter. I started and stopped and started again, but I knew it was only going to happen if I did it – and just wishing for it to be done wasn't going to accomplish anything. I had to follow through with the work, and gradually, doubt faded away.

Think of a giant scale in your life with your goal on one side and doubt on the other. You are the only person who can change the way the scale tips, and you must do that by taking action. Action will help you take the weight off of the doubt side and start adding weight to the goal side. It may take a long time, but intentional action will help you gradually tip the scales.

Focus on Faith

"It's time"...The words rang in my ears and felt like a sucker punch to the stomach. I hung up the phone slowly from talking to my uncle. Mack and I had driven down to Florida for a getaway weekend for the holiday to do some mountain biking. I didn't want to tell him we had to go home. We had already paid for our entire hotel stay and leaving today would mean cutting it short. I knew he needed a few days of rest as much as I did. But, I couldn't stay away when the hospice nurse told them to call in the family because my great grandmother had reached the end of her earthly time.

We drove almost non-stop on the way home. I didn't care. I was already grieving. I knew it was coming. I knew it was coming 4 weeks before when Granny fell and x-rays showed some fractures, either from the fall or just because her body was breaking down. She stayed in a nursing home for a few days, and I went to see her. I knew then, the end was coming.

My grandmother greeted me at the door when we drove up after 10:00pm. "You are just in time." she said, taking my hand and hugging me hard. I made my way quietly down the hall to Granny's room where she lay, breathing with such difficulty. I barely recognized her. She had lost so much weight since seeing her a few days before, and she had lost the ability to speak to us.

Tears came without my permission, but I couldn't help it. Leonardo da Vinci said, *"Tears come from the heart and not the brain."* My heart knew her life was ending. It was a peaceful ending, a release to something better. In my mind, I knew she had impacted my life and my faith in a way no one else had done. It didn't matter how bad she was hurting, she would always say, "Thank God it's as good as it is."

I held her hand, and for a precious time, I sang hymns to her as she passed away. I sang the songs we sang when I was growing up as she taught me the words. We would sit in the swing in the backyard or walk around the block and sing praise songs. That night, I was so distraught I forgot some of the words, but I just kept singing and humming when I had to. I know her heart heard me.

Granny's faith in God never waivered, regardless of what she was facing. She never seemed to question God or His plan for her. If she ever doubted, I never knew it. Her faith was more than the size of a mustard seed that could move mountains. It was the size of the mountain itself, and faith had seen her through everything.

The opposite of doubt is faith. It's trusting in something and believing in the outcome, even when you don't have "proof." Max De Pree said, "*We cannot become what we need to be by remaining what we are.*" God gives us challenges to overcome because they make us stronger, more determined, and more faithful.

I know the easy times in life have taught me very little, but the difficult times in life have given me new strength and faith in God's purpose. I can't promise you will always understand God's purpose and plan, but I can tell you He will use the trials in life for good. It may never happen or years may go by before you can look back and see how the trials in life have helped you be stronger, better, tougher, and more determined.

Questions for Contemplation or Group Discussion

1. How are you letting doubt take control of your life right now?

2. What action steps do you know you need to take but haven't yet? What's holding you back?

3. Who in your life is a role model of faith?

4. Who is looking at you as a role model? How can you be a better role model?

5. Read, reflect and/or discuss these bible verses: James 1:5-8; Matthew 14:31; Matthew 21:21; 2 Timothy 1:7

RIA STORY

Chapter Seven
NOT ASHAMED OF MY SHAME

"Hardship often prepares an ordinary person for an extraordinary destiny."

C.S. Lewis

I consider myself to be something of a shame expert. After all, I live with it, even today, as I expect most of us victims of child/teenage sexual abuse do. And, I believe God is perhaps the only One who can help me heal from shame. Not guilt, but shame.

In her book, *Daring Greatly*, Brené Brown defines guilt as a feeling about one's actions and shame as a feeling about one's self (What I did was terrible, guilt, versus what I am is terrible, shame). Guilt can be an emotion to drive us to change our behavior and can be used positively. Shame only brings negative emotions because it's an emotion based on your opinion of yourself and who or what you are.

I was 12 when my dad started doing and saying things to me he shouldn't have. I was taught to be a people pleaser. I wasn't capable of making adult decisions, and like most twelve-year-old little girls, I hero-worshipped my dad. If he told me I could help him, then that's exactly what I wanted to do – even though deep inside I knew something was not right about it since we had to keep it a secret. You can't feel good about yourself when you are doing things you aren't proud of.

Even today, I carry a sense of shame, even though

it's not logical. I was just a child, and I KNOW all of that. But, it's still there. Knowing and feeling are two very different things. Even today, I work hard to control my thoughts and feelings in this area of my past.

When fighting this battle, it's important to admit our feelings and acknowledge them. Then, we can begin to heal. Because I can say, "Yes, there is a sense of shame," I can acknowledge that feeling and reason out why I should not feel that way. And then, I have ammunition when that little voice in my head wants to tell me I don't deserve happiness today because I'm a terrible person who did terrible things. I fight the feeling of not wanting to be known as a victim of abuse.

Shame is a funny thing – it gets stronger when we don't acknowledge it and holds more power over us simply because we don't want to admit it.

If I feel shame about who or what I am, then I can only heal from that if I change who or what I am. It's something I struggle with even with God's help – I can't imagine doing it alone. The redemption offered to us through Jesus is the only way to completely change who and what we are inside because He offers us redemption we cannot find anywhere else. I can't imagine fighting a shame battle without Him.

Self-worth

In the late spring months of 2000, I sat in the armchair in front of my computer. I listened carefully to make sure I heard the sound of dad driving off. I knew when he was gone I could escape to a book or my online friends and pretend to forget, for a little while, the horrible truth of my life.

Dad being gone meant privacy, and I treasured any opportunity to have it. I always felt like I didn't have any control over my life. I always felt like he invaded my right to have physical privacy. Of course, since he was so involved with me sexually, he knew far more than I would have been comfortable with anyone knowing, much less my dad. I had resorted to putting towels underneath the door in the bathroom because he told me once he would watch me in the tub bathing from underneath the doorjamb. I became more and more secretive with anything I could control. I would ride my horse for hours at a time and not tell anyone where I went, sometimes just riding into a hiding place in the woods to read in peace.

As I heard the sound of the truck fade away, it hit me. I hated living a life full of lies and deception. I felt like I had three lives instead of one – the public Ria my family and friends knew, the secret Ria that lived for the escape, that however unhealthy, she found where she could; and the shameful Ria, the one that was so sinful she was performing sexual activities every night with her dad, so he could "train" her to be a wife. His wife.

Rather than turn on the computer or find a novel, I just sat there. I could picture ten years into the future and nothing would have changed. I wasn't ever going to truly date anyone or walk down the aisle toward a husband. I wasn't ever going to be able to live without being ashamed of what happened in my bedroom every night. I wasn't ever going to forget that. When it came down to it, I was able to do what it took to survive and bury the part of me that wanted to scream "No!" when told what I would have to do to earn horse feed for my horses.

"I am so messed up!" I told myself. Why bother with going on? It wasn't going to change. What was the point in continuing to live like a prisoner in the home I grew up in? This wasn't really living. I wouldn't have been able to describe self-worth at that moment, but I didn't have any. All I knew was the future looked so bleak I didn't want to continue.

I had seen movies and read books where someone committed suicide. I knew cutting your wrists was supposed to be relatively painless, and I even knew where the razor blades were in dad's toolbox. It sounded like such a *reasonable* solution at that moment. I didn't want to live through another ten years of the misery I was living in; most of it, I felt, was my own fault. Only someone who was as awful as I was would be in the situation I was in.

Of course, there were some good times. On the surface, I lived a good life. But, so often, we don't truly know what a person is going through. Sometimes, we don't want to know. So, we don't ask.

I'm not really sure what kept me from following through that day. That's not true – I am sure. It was God's intervention because there wasn't anything else to stop me. I like to think a little angel named hope came and sat on my shoulder to whisper to me.

When we lose our sense of self worth, we feel like we are worthless, and therefore, have no value. When we feel like our life has no value or meaning, we question why we should continue living. Why go through the motions for nothing? Sometimes, we just feel too tired, and it feels like too much effort for nothing.

I would love to tell you I woke up the next morning and everything was instantly better. That wouldn't be true.

It's a slow climb out of a deep hole we dig for ourselves. Even when we feel like no one loves us or cares about us, remember, God does. Remember, even if you feel shame because of things you have done in the past, you can change things going forward.

Self-talk

Daniel Goleman tells us "Self awareness is recognizing a feeling as it happens." It's important to first KNOW your emotions and what you are feeling, so you can then change it. You can change your feelings. It's not easy sometimes, but it can be done. How? Change your thoughts. Change what you tell yourself - your self-talk.

You are the most important person you will talk to because you listen to yourself. There is no filter when it comes to the things we tell our inner self, so it's too easy to believe what we tell ourselves, good and bad.

In his book, *Biology of Belief*, Bruce Lipton says, "*I call it the belief effect to stress that our perceptions, whether they are accurate or inaccurate, equally impact our behavior and our bodies.*"

He goes on to say, we don't know enough about how powerful the mind can be in healing itself and the body. He references a study that demonstrates how incredibly the mind can convince itself of something. In the study, three groups of patients were suffering from knee pain. For the first group, a surgeon performed surgery and shaved out cartilage from the knee. For the second group, he flushed out the knee joint to remove some material from the knee. The third group got "fake surgery" where the surgeon made an incision while the patient was sedated. He talked and acted exactly like he was performing the surgery, and then, sewed up the incisions.

All three groups received the same postoperative care, including exercise. The first two groups improved, but shockingly, the third group experienced just as much improvement as the first two!

I remember when I started mountain bike racing in 2011 and how I crashed frequently. It wasn't unusual to fall or wreck at least once every time Mack and I went riding. When I started competing and trying to go faster, it got worse. I wasn't a naturally gifted athlete, and after all, I had grown up riding horses not bikes.

One race demonstrated the power of self-talk to me. It was on a very "technical" trail, meaning there was a lot of rocks and roots and tricky sections of the trail to navigate. It was a short race loop. We would have to run the same loop three times over the course of the race, and I had my share of wrecks.

The worst part of the trail was a bridge over a creek because the "bridge" was only about 12" wide. The creek was several feet down. If you ran off the "bridge," it would be a long drop to the creek bed. Each and every time we had practiced riding this trail, I would get off my bike and walk across the bridge. I refused to even try to ride it, telling myself I would just ride off it and wreck. Mack would zip along and then have to stop and wait while I would dismount and carefully walk, carrying my bike across.

Race day came, and I dreaded it. I didn't want to look at that bridge, much less have to consider whether I would try to ride it or not. I completed the first two laps of the race loop, and I was in first place. I knew it was costing me a lot of time to walk across instead of riding each time I got to the bridge. The second time, I told myself I wasn't going to get off when I got to it on my third lap. I spent the next five miles talking to myself and telling myself how easy it would be to simply ride a straight line. I wasn't going to think about the bridge or the fact there was nothing to catch me. I knew I could ride in a straight line, and that's all I really had to do.

When I came around the turn and saw the bridge ahead, I didn't even hesitate or slow down. I lined up straight on and looked ahead down the trail. I never once let myself look down at the narrow bridge or the creek, focusing instead on riding straight across. It worked – to my incredible surprise. I realized I had the skills to ride it, but I had lacked the belief in myself. I had talked myself out of trying. Worse – I believed myself! There wasn't anyone else in my head to tell me I could do it, and that's why we have to be careful what we tell ourselves.

Self-love

I wake each morning and reach for my glasses before I even get out of bed. I'm extremely near-sighted. I cannot even see to read my computer screen without my glasses or contacts. Without them, driving would be impossible. Even walking around without glasses or contacts is hazardous to my health. I put my glasses on, and the world becomes clear. Everything comes into focus, and the world becomes beautiful. It's not that everything changes, but my focus becomes clear. I see things as they truly are.

Our perception of inner-self is much like me looking at the world without glasses. How often we see, and judge, ourselves without a true focus on what we really look like inside.

Sometimes, we judge ourselves better than we truly are. We judge ourselves by our good intentions, rather than our actions. To avoid this, it's important to be completely honest when reflecting on your inner values.

Your internal values, or what you truly value in your heart, will determine your thoughts, words and actions.

Sometimes, we judge ourselves much harder than we should. We judge ourselves by the self-defeating thoughts that come creeping in. We carry around guilt or shame from something and allow it to spoil the rest of our lives. Guilt is negative feelings about one's actions: "I made a mistake," while shame is negative feelings about one's self: "I am a mistake."

When I feel a sense of shame or worthlessness creeping in, I stop and redirect my thoughts.

The all time classic book, *"As A Man Thinketh"* by James Allen is a small volume of life-changing wisdom. My mentor, John Maxwell, read this book when he was 17 for the first time, and he has read it once a year, every year, since then. I thought it must certainly be an important book if it was worth re-reading every year by someone like John Maxwell, so I ordered it.

When the book arrived, I was shocked at how *small* it was, 38 pages, and that includes the forward page and the title page. This was the book that bears reading and re-reading, year after year? At least, it was short. I guess if you are going to read something over and over again, short is good.

I quickly read through it, and then, I read it again. I realized it is a life-changing book if it is understood and applied. The title of the book is based off of Proverbs 23, *"As a man thinketh in his heart, so is he."* (Proverbs 23:7) One of the passages I have underlined in red, reads: *"The soul attracts that which it secretly harbors; that which it loves, and also that which it fears.... Good thoughts bear good fruit, bad thoughts bad fruit."*

I want to think good thoughts that will bear good fruit. It's not easy to do sometimes.

I know all about the self-defeating thoughts, the self-loathing, the guilt, and the shame that can go through our heads sometimes. I know about looking in the mirror and not loving the me that looks back.

What I've learned is that self-love means loving all of me. Self-love means loving the me in the mirror, even the broken parts. Self-love means seeing me for who I am, including the flaws, and loving me anyway. Self-love means taking care of the me in the mirror. Not just physically, although that's important, but also emotionally and spiritually.

Self-love means valuing ourselves. When we value ourselves, we will treasure our time, talents, thoughts, and abilities. When we value our time, talents, thoughts, and abilities, we won't waste them, but use them wisely. Self-love is being a good steward of the gift of life.

Self-love means loving even the broken bits and pieces because they are still part of me, and they form the whole. Self-love means seeing ourselves as God sees us, imperfect, yet still a beautiful creature with a purpose for living. Self-love is seeing yourself with a clear focus. Accept the flaws that you cannot change, and work to improve on the things you can.

I have found having a bad day would make me much more likely to find something sugary sweet to eat in the cabinet, or maybe, I would turn to food to find comfort. Then, I felt even worse because I knew I ate too much and felt worse not just physically, but also emotionally, because I would then beat myself up over my choices.

Rather than travel that road, I realized the power of making a good choice to start with and that begins with thinking the right thoughts. I found when I want something, if I stop and ask myself why I want it and why I would be eating it, it helps me make a better decision. I think about eating it, how I would feel afterward, and what I would gain from eating it. Focusing more on fueling my brain and body causes me to value different outcomes than the immediate urge to have some chocolate.

Coffee is another example – I love coffee simply because it tastes good, but I limit how much of it I drink because I know too much caffeine isn't good for me and affects my sleep. I also quit adding sugar and artificial creamer and enjoy the coffee itself, not the sweet creamy concoctions I used to call coffee.

I must say here the battle of eating well and exercising was a tough one for me in the past. I struggled with making poor food choices and then exercising too much in the effort to balance it out or to regain a sense of control. Rest days and balance are now an important part of my life because I realize being out of balance in one area will cause life to be out of balance in another.

We can become addicted to anything. Even healthy behaviors can become unhealthy addictions. It's important we are conscious of what we do and why we are doing it. When we have a strong sense of self-worth and self-love, we will be more conscious of our choices each day and make better choices.

It's like flexing a mind-muscle. Self-discipline in this area gets easier if you practice it more often. I also realize I don't have to get it right 100% of the time. I can enjoy what I eat and treat myself sometimes, but I choose carefully when and how.

If I don't love myself, I won't care for, or about, myself. Once I realized that, a lot of difficult choices became easy. Now, a healthy and well balanced diet is easy because I love myself, and I want to take care of my physical body. Sure, I love ice cream and pizza as much as anyone, but I am careful to not overindulge because I realize what I eat affects my physical health. Not only that, if I'm physically healthy, I have a head start on emotional wellness too.

I absolutely love exercise because it helps me take care of my health in so many ways. I love to get outside and hike, bike, walk, or run. I love to take a class or teach one at the gym. There are times I am not able to do any of those activities. I must force myself to get on the treadmill or elliptical trainer, which I don't enjoy. I do it because I know it's important to exercise regularly, and sometimes, that's the only option available.

Because I value myself, I invest in myself, not just physically, but mentally. One of my goals for 2015 was to read 50 non-fiction books to help me develop my mind. I've already chosen most of the books I will read in 2016 and already have nearly 50 books on my list. My Amazon budget is more than my annual clothes budget.

Loving one's self doesn't mean we pretend to be perfect or without error, but it does mean accepting and loving one's self as a creation of God. I choose to accept me for who I am and realize God created me. I'm not perfect, but I'm His and with that comes forgiveness, redemption, and perfect peace, knowing God knows who and what I am, and He still loves me – so I should too.

Questions for Contemplation or Group Discussion

1. What affirmations could you use to remember you are a special person created by God for a special purpose that only you can fulfill?

2. What experiences in your past do you need to give over to God? It's time to let go of being ashamed of them.

3. What thoughts do you tell yourself every day that help build your sense of self-worth? What thoughts do you tell yourself every day that don't? What needs to change?

4. Read, reflect and/or discuss these bible verses: Psalm 25:2; Isaiah 50:7; Isaiah 54:4; Hebrews 12:2

Chapter Eight
LIVING WITH COURAGE

"Death is not the greatest loss in life. The greatest loss is what dies inside us while we live."

Norman Cousins

I attend a weekly fellowship gathering where, each week, someone who is local to the area and wants to share what God has done in his or her life shares a different testimony. It's an incredible gathering because every person there shares a wonder of God and His power. I've heard stories of redemption, recovery, and forgiveness, and I've heard stories of triumph over pain and past. I was blessed and humbled to share my own story of how God has used the pain from my past for His purpose.

This is where I heard Joe Castillo speak and watched him draw. Joe has a strong message of forgiveness and a very powerful message of how holding on to bitterness in life will only poison one's self.

The meeting always breaks up slowly after the speaker finishes, and everyone in the room connects with people they know, some they don't know, and some they want to know better. Recently, a man I have met a few times came up to me, and we spoke a few minutes. He then shared with me a message God had laid on his heart, and it touched me.

It touched me so much that, in spite of myself, I couldn't hold back the tears. He immediately apologized.

I'm sure he had no idea I would become emotional. I had to assure him, it wasn't his fault, nor was there anything wrong in what he said. I simply cry easily these days. However, I also laugh easily these days, more than ever before. I remember an old Patty Loveless song chorus: "It's okay to hurt, and it's okay to cry." For a long time after leaving my home, my parents, and my brother behind, I didn't truly believe it was okay to hurt.

Since 2013 when I started sharing my story, I'm so much more in tune with my emotions, and I allow myself to feel them. I've realized how wonderful it is to be able to (appropriately) enjoy the emotions God gives us. I am more "alive" than I ever have been. I've learned to be vulnerable as I share my story of overcoming years of abuse.

I let go of the shame, guilt, and secrecy of the past and learned to be more alive as a result. I'm truly free, and it's a wonderful blessing. It's not that I didn't laugh over the years, but I had learned to numb such a large part of myself because I didn't know how else to cope. I thought simply burying the past was the best way to go on with life. So, I did. I buried it, locked it up, and threw away the key, numbing my pain, but also my joy in life.

We can't numb only part of our vulnerability. In the words of Brené Brown, "*Numbing vulnerability also dulls our experiences of love, joy, belonging, creativity, and empathy. We can't selectively numb emotion. Numb the dark and you numb the light.*"

Rather than bury our feelings, what would it be like to acknowledge them as part of us, examine them, why we have them, and then take action (or not) based on them? Does it hurt sometimes? Yes, of course. But, would you trade feeling the joy, so you don't have to feel the pain? It's much like when someone makes a decision to get a pet, a dog or a cat you expect will not live as long as you do – and yet, it's worth the loss you will at some point feel. Or, the decision to get married – sooner or later you will have a fight, and it won't be pretty. But, would you want to live your entire life alone simply to avoid that?

Truly living means to be alive. To be alive means sometimes we laugh, sometimes we love, sometimes we hurt, and sometimes we cry. And, that's okay. It takes courage to be vulnerable. It takes courage to learn to live life like it was meant to be lived.

The Courage To Reach Your Potential

When I didn't get to make decisions for myself, I didn't have to think about them. It wasn't that I had never thought for myself, I just had not had the freedom to act on those thoughts when living with my parents. Of course, children and teenagers need guidance and counsel. But at 19, I wasn't allowed to do anything outside the home without my dad's approval. Even when I went out somewhere, I had to be careful "not to talk to any guys" because dad didn't want me to. I was supposed to give dad an exact plan of where I was going, who I was going with, and what we were doing. If the plan changed, I was supposed to call and make sure he knew. As long as it was an approved activity, he let me do things. But, I had to beg, plead, and bargain for the privilege. And, he called it just that, a privilege to do something. It was always clear I was allowed to go or do something only because of his good graces.

The constant pressure of living like a virtual prisoner was heavy and weighed on me. Like almost any teenager, I longed for some freedom. I didn't realize it was unreasonable to not have any at all.

Sudden freedom...liberation. It took me a little while to realize after leaving home, I was free. I no longer had to ask someone for permission to go somewhere like the library or the grocery store. I no longer had to worry about being home at a certain time of day. I didn't have to beg for permission to have lunch with a friend. Once I started working, I didn't even have to ask someone if I could spend money.

It was rather exciting to go to the store and buy something myself. I remember coming home one day and showing Mack the new floor mats I had bought for our Blazer. They weren't fancy or expensive or anything, just some rubber floor mats to keep the carpet from getting ruined during my trips to the barn. I didn't even ask him before I purchased them. I realized I didn't have to. I realized I wasn't dependent on someone for everything.

It was...scary.

After leaving my parents' home, I realized making decisions for myself meant more than just planning out the grocery list for the week. I had to decide where I wanted to go in life. It didn't take long to decide working as a waitress wasn't going to be what I wanted to do the rest of my life. It was honest work, and I was proud to have it. But, I didn't want to do it forever. Let's face it – bussing tables for dollar tips isn't glamorous, and no one dreams about growing up to pick up half-eaten pizza crusts off the floor.

The most difficult thing about making my own decisions was the possibility of failure. For example, I realized I needed to get my GED since I didn't have a high school diploma. The process itself isn't complicated – you register to take the exam and show up.

The scary part was facing the fact I was going to try

to do something new and realizing there was a possibility I might not pass. What if I failed? What if I had to try again? So much of my self-worth at that point was tied to achieving. I felt tremendous pressure to prove to Mack, and everyone else, I was capable of something and could overcome my past.

I knew I wanted to work at the hospital, and I knew I had to go to school to do it. But, what if I wasn't good in school? I had never attended a traditional school, and I had never been in a classroom setting.

I didn't even know how to talk to people very well. The thought of an entire room of people I didn't know terrified me. People ask questions, and I didn't know how I would answer them. Or, I didn't want to answer them. I had too much in my past I was ashamed of.

How do you tell a college counselor you don't really know what you want to do or what degree you want because you have only just now realized you have options.

How do you explain you aren't sure you can do anything because you never have done anything by the world's standards? I wasn't comfortable having a dinner conversation, much less responding well in a job interview.

All too often, we play small in life. We settle. We get comfortable. It's safer, and really, who wants to play big and risk failure?

I faced fear like that head on again when I felt the tug of potential pulling me to pursue being a speaker. By that time, I was working in a job I was happy in at a great organization where I considered my co-workers almost like family. And yet, there was this pull, this thought, this dream that God had a different path for me. I felt the temptation to ignore it. Play safe. Stay comfortable.

Forget the dream. I could avoid the fear of stepping out into the unknown by simply saying "No." It would have been easy to avoid the risk of stepping into the scary world of self-employment, expensive individual insurance policies, and no 401K matching.

We've all faced opportunities in life and perhaps made the wrong decision because of fear of failure. Perhaps, you are facing a decision right now about your career or your goals this year and the possibility of failure is staring you down. So, you make the easy choice or don't make a choice at all, which is the same thing.

And, that's okay. Perhaps, you don't want to do, have, and be more in life - it's not for everyone. I know that. I'm not here to blame you or point fingers at anyone who chooses to play it safe. But, if you have the potential for MORE and are ready to take a step towards it, the first step is to acknowledge the fear. It's okay to be afraid. Being brave is being afraid and doing it anyway.

Ask yourself if you are seeing any of the following three signs you might be playing it safe, settling for less, or playing too small in the game of life. Decide if you need to do something about it – and then do it. Do it afraid. Do it with bravery. Do it with courage.

1) You lack energy, enthusiasm, and excitement for your job or work:

You wake up to the sound of the alarm clock and your first thought is "Ugh. It's morning again. Time to get up and drag myself through the day." You don't really look forward to going to work, in fact, you really wish it was Saturday, and you were off. You can't wait to chill out in front of the T.V. tonight and escape all those pesky emails from your co-workers and those piles of papers on your desk. It's time to ask yourself - what are you truly passionate about and how can you live your dream instead of dreaming to live?

2) You thought those little quirks weren't a big deal - but they are:

Maybe, it's not work you dread, but coming home afterward. You don't really want to ask, "How was your day?" because you don't really want to know. It started as the perfect match, and you were willing to put up with him leaving his dirty socks on the floor or her habit of hitting the snooze button 10 times in the morning. You had high hopes for this relationship and thought you would be able to help your significant other change (for the better of course).

But, now you realize, they don't want to change - they like who they are. It's time to have an honest talk about what each of you expects from and is willing to invest in the relationship.

3) You feel little satisfaction or find no meaning in what you do:

It feels like it's meaningless. You don't feel like you are making a difference to anyone and wonder if anyone would miss you when you are gone. Oh sure, they would miss you for a while, but the organization would go on without you and really wouldn't change much if you weren't there. You get to work, go to the meetings, meet the deadlines (or don't), but you feel like you aren't really making an IMPACT on anyone. No one's life is changed for the better because you are there today.

Or perhaps, you do make a difference but feel like something is missing somehow. You are completely competent and do the job well, but it doesn't give you that satisfaction you see other people find when completing a job well done. It's time to discover your purpose in life.

Our deepest fear is that we can do, have, and be more because that would require us to step out and do something about it. If we embrace the chance of living life to the fullest, we must be willing to accept responsibility for doing it.

The Courage To Be Free

I tried very hard to ignore what happened to me. I didn't want to talk about it. I didn't want to talk about my parents. I hated questions from well meaning acquaintances about how my parents were doing or where they were living now.

How do you tell someone you have just met you don't talk to your parents because your dad abused you for seven years, and your mom blames you for it?

How do you tell someone from the church where your parents grew up you don't speak to your dad because he used you for sex and shared you with other men?

How do you answer when someone asks about your brother, but you haven't seen him in years? You never got to tell him why you were leaving home, and you don't know if he hates you for tearing his family apart.

I thought if I didn't talk about it, maybe I would forget. I didn't want to remember. I wasn't truly free. Breaking free of something means you aren't in bondage any longer. I was still in bondage, even though I didn't admit it.

It took time to learn to be truly free. I didn't find freedom until I realized my past shaped me, refining rather than defining the person I am today. I had to learn to embrace that, accept it, and refuse to be pitied for it. When someone learns of my past today and says, "I'm sorry," I have learned to say, "It's okay – God doesn't cause the pain in life. He uses it for His purpose, and I'm blessed to be living free today."

Two years ago, I spoke in Orlando to more than 700 people at a conference. I gave a three-minute speech about attitude and told my story to share that we can't choose what happens to us, but we can choose how we respond. It was one of the first times I had spoken to a large group about my personal story, and I had worked for months to prepare. After speaking, so many people, men and women, shared a similar story with me. They all touched my heart with their stories, and it was humbling to hear how God had helped them see a new perspective of their experiences through me.

One woman in particular moved me to tears. She found me in the crowd and shared her own story. She was from a small country and had been raped at age 17 by a prominent man in the community. She became pregnant, but no one believed her when she named her rapist because he was a local leader and a married man. She was shunned, even by her own family, and eventually shipped off to a relative in another country because she brought shame to her family. Eventually, she immigrated to the United States where she raised her son and went on to be a physician in a successful medical practice. She told no one of the circumstances related to her son's conception, carrying the guilt for more than 20 years, until she heard me speak on stage. She was crying with tears of joy streaming down her face as she hugged me fiercely.

"Ria, you have given me wings, and I will fly! I will

be free now! Free of the past. Free of the burden! You have helped me see it was not my fault. I will not be shamed any longer!"

I get chill bumps when I think of how God is able to use me to share His message and to help others, and it helps me to see even though God doesn't cause the pain in our lives, He is able to use it to shape our lives.

It takes courage to live each day refusing to be in bondage to our past experiences and mistakes. We can choose to move forward by acknowledging the past and learning from it.

It's still scary at times to live free and let go of the past. As Robert Morris says, *"We're only as free as our minds are."*

Questions for Contemplation or Group Discussion

1. What are you passionate about? What is your purpose in life? Are you in alignment with your passion and purpose?

2. What would you attempt to do if you knew you would not fail?

3. What do you dream about doing that you aren't doing now? What needs to happen in order for you to be able to do it?

4. If you recognize any of the warning signs in your life, what steps will you take toward realizing your potential?

5. What do you need to let go of from your past? What burdens do you need to lay down?

6. What can you learn from a mistake you made in the past?

7. Read, reflect and/or discuss these bible verses: Deuteronomy 31:6; 1 Corinthians 13:16; Psalm 31:24; Isaiah 40:31

RIA STORY

Chapter Nine
THE LEADER IN YOU

"If your actions inspire others to dream more, learn more, do more, and become more, you are a leader."

John Quincy Adams

I know some of you are asking, "Why is there a chapter on leadership in a book about resilience?" Leadership is influence, and we all have influence over others and ourselves. To be effective is to be intentional about the way we influence self and others.

Leadership. It's one of the most misunderstood words in the professional world, and perhaps in the personal development world. Anytime we talk about resilience, attitude, positivity, self-discipline, and so on, we are talking about influence of self. When we talk about teamwork, communication, and relationships, we are talking about influence of others.

John Maxwell said, "*Leadership is influence. Nothing more. Nothing less.*" So often, we have the idea that leadership is only for those people who are managers, directors, or bosses. There is a common perception leadership isn't important unless you are in a formal position with a title and authority over other people. But, leadership isn't just for those people. Although it's important for those in the formal role of leader, leadership is for everyone because we are all leaders.

Donald McGannon noted, "*Leadership is action, not position.*" I didn't always understand that. There was a time in my life where I couldn't wait to be the boss, so I could be the leader. I didn't realize I was already a leader, even though I didn't have a title that said "Boss." When I finally got the title, it didn't make me a better leader.

In 2007, I had just been promoted to office manager at a busy physician practice. I had worked there for several years and the previous two office managers had been terminated, which should have told me something about the job I was getting into. I immediately wanted to make some changes around the office, including rearranging some things at the front desk to improve efficiency, and help solve the bottleneck of patients checking in at the front desk. I failed to get buy-in from everyone involved in the process first however, thinking since I was the boss, I could simply make a command decision.

It didn't work. After only one morning of working with the new check-in process, one of the physicians flatly refused to continue. It started out great. Those working the front desk loved it because it made their job so much faster. However, one of the physicians said changing the check-in process caused him to get behind in seeing patients because he couldn't tell if there was a backlog at the front desk. He demanded we return to the old way of doing things. So, we did. It was the first of many learning opportunities in my job there as I "failed forward" in developing my leadership skills. I learned a painful, but very valuable, lesson about developing influence with those I worked with. I also learned about getting buy-in before making decisions that affect others.

We all want to influence someone: spouses, children, bosses, parents, friends, co-workers, the clerk ringing up your groceries, and in fact, almost anyone we meet. If we influence them positively, we are good leaders. If we influence them negatively, we are poor leaders. If we don't influence them much, we are ineffective leaders.

Development of your leadership skills will help you to become more effective in everything else. Better leadership skills will allow you to be more effective as a parent, a spouse, a friend, a boss, a manager, a follower, or any other "hat" you are wearing. Because leadership skills are the skills we need to influence people.

We all want and need leadership skills, or influence skills. However, it's not enough to simply want leadership skills. They must be developed over time with intentional creation of habits that help us build influence. We should study leadership with as much, or perhaps more, emphasis as we put on learning to do the technical component of any role. Our leadership skills, or the lack of them, will determine whether the people around us are the greatest asset or the biggest challenge.

Leadership of Yourself

Leadership of others starts with leadership of self. We must have the capacity to influence our self first, before we can begin to build the ability to influence others. It starts within. This means influencing ourselves in both a physical and mental way. First by developing our influence over self. Then, by developing influence with others.

To improve our influence over self and others, we must develop our character, or who we are inside. In his book, *Blue-Collar Leadership: Leading from the Front Lines*, Mack Story (my favorite leadership expert!) defines character as: *"thinking, feeling, and acting in a congruent way while making excellent moral and ethical choices based on self-*

evident natural laws and principles."

In 2015, I was at a leadership conference and John Maxwell was speaking. He was teaching on mentoring and how it can be a valuable tool when done appropriately. He believes in mentoring others and is very selective of the people whom he chooses to invest his time in. What I found most interesting however, wasn't what he shared about how he mentors others, but the fact he has mentors himself. In fact, he shared there are six areas of his life where he seeks a mentor: 1) Faith 2) Relationships 3) Equipping Others 4) Thinking 5) Leadership and 6) Health. (Yes, the number one leadership expert in the world is still learning leadership from others.)

He shared with us all that he struggled with making healthy life choices, so he is now very intentional about seeking help in that area of his life. He talked about having a personal trainer and nutritionist because he KNOWS he doesn't lead himself in that area as well as he should. He has taken a very deliberate and intentional action to ensure he has the help and support needed to influence his choices. He has found a way to lead himself better in the area of physical health. He pointed out none of us do everything well. The key is recognizing where you need help, mentoring, or coaching, and then getting it.

What is interesting is after he shared that with us all, he influenced many people there to become more intentional about their own physical health. John influenced himself first, and then he influenced many others. But, notice he had to do it first – we can't give someone what we don't have.

What I want to point out is this: until we can lead ourselves well, we aren't equipped to lead someone else.

We first must lead ourselves – both physically and mentally. Physically, we should take care of the vessel God gave us to fulfill His purpose for our life. Mentally, we should develop the brain God gave us to fulfill His purpose for our lives.

I've learned it's not the lack of knowledge that holds us back – it's the application. That's one of the reasons I am so passionate about coaching – because it helps the individual identify what's holding them back and how they can overcome it – in their own way. Coaching isn't prescriptive – I can't tell someone how to live their life, but I can help them figure out how to live their life better.

Leadership starts within. In his book, *The 7 Habits of Highly Effective People,* Stephen R. Covey talks about the four dimensions: Physical, mental, social, and spiritual. Notice, three of them deal with self, and only one actually involves others. That's because we must start with self.

When Mack and I were traveled to Guatemala as part of a team of John Maxwell Team Coaches participating in a cultural transformation of Guatemala. We were facilitating leadership roundtables with leaders in the country from all seven streams of influence. It was incredible because it helped me realize the significant difference I could make in the lives of others. Paired with an interpreter, I was able to visit several different organizations and teach leadership principles to many people over the course of the week. The theme of the cultural transformation: "Transformation begins with me."

That week, our team taught over 20,000 people one core value – transformation of a nation begins with transformation of the individual. Transform enough individuals and you will transform the nation. Or, the company, church, classroom, or community. But, it starts with each person. I can't change anyone else – I can only change me. When we quit trying to make everyone else better and start focusing our improvement efforts internally, then and only then, we will see transformation.

I was flipping through an old scrapbook last year, looking for pictures to include in my book, *Ria's Story From Ashes To Beauty*. I found a few, but I also found something else that caught my attention. It was sort of a letter to myself, a list of character traits I compiled when I was about 11 or 12. I wanted to have these qualities as an adult. I thought it was so important I wrote out the list by hand and taped it into my scrapbook as a keepsake. What a strange feeling to come across this list as an adult and ask myself, how many of those traits do I truly have today?

I still value those character traits, perhaps even more so today as I realize the struggle to be true to my ideal. I've learned the most difficult person to influence and lead is one's self!

Leadership of Others

When we start developing the skills, thinking, and habits of the person we want to become, we are preparing to become that person. We can't wait for the opportunity before we start preparing. If we wait to develop our leadership skills, we may never get the opportunity to be in a leadership position because we won't be prepared. Preparation must happen first, so opportunity can present itself. Bobby Unser noted, *"Success is where preparation and opportunity meet."*

We start by developing the critical skills we need to interact with others. Communication skills, conversation skills, and the ability to increase our influence with others are keys to success. Think of almost any project worth doing, whether at church, at work, or in the community. They all have one thing in common – your ability to get results will be determined by your ability to influence and lead others to accomplish the mission.

Leadership and influence is like respect – it can only be earned, not demanded. A formal position of authority actually has very little to do with our leadership and influence. If we wait until we are in a formal position of authority to start developing as a leader, then we may never get there, and if we do, we won't be effective as leaders. Mark Miller said, *"You can lead with or without a title. If you wait until you get a title, you may wait forever."*

We overestimate the amount of control that comes with being at the top. Until you are in a position of authority at the top, you believe things would be different if you were in control. It's not until you start going higher you realize it still comes down to influence, and influence doesn't automatically happen with a position.

We should strive to reach our potential rather than the top of the organization. Focusing on reaching the top of an organization will limit opportunities. Focusing on growth will expand opportunities. The majority of people will make more of an impact from somewhere other than the top.

You can make an impact from wherever you are in an organization. You don't have to be the top leader to be a leader and make a difference. We can all add value right where we are, and while helping others, we will help ourselves. If we refuse to become a leader because we don't believe we can get to the top, we are limiting ourselves from reaching our potential, and we are limiting the impact we can have on others.

Questions for Contemplation or Group Discussion

1. Who are the people in your life that you influence? Is your influence positive or negative?

2. How would life be different if you had more influence? How would your family be different? How would work be different?

3. What are some ways you can increase your leadership skills? What will you do each day to improve yourself and your character?

4. Name some leaders in the bible. What made them effective as leaders?

5. Read, reflect and/or discuss these bible verses: Matthew 6:1 – 7:27; Mark 8:34-38

Chapter Ten
THE PERFECTION OF PEACE

"Peace is a journey of a thousand miles and it must be taken one step at a time."

Lyndon B. Johnson

Today is a Gift – Don't Waste It Looking Back

"Needs a good home." You skim across these posts when you see them on Facebook. You see the homemade fliers on the community bulletin board and ignore them.

Someone has found an abandoned or lost dog or cat and wants to make sure they have a home instead of taking it to the pound. Or perhaps, someone has to part with a beloved pet and wants to ensure the pet is cared for.

A cute photo always accompanies the "ad" and frequently the animal comes with some requirements: Needs kind owner, has been abused, loves kids, doesn't like men, needs lots of TLC, would make a great pet for an older person, etc. I know the feeling. No, not the feeling of the person who found the animal – I know the feelings the animal would have if it could talk. In 2000, my ad would have read something like this:

Needs A Good Home: Broken, 19 year old girl – abused and traumatized for years; needs compassion and understanding; needs kind words, gentleness and love; requires lots of hugs; comes with some risk – former owner may try to repossess by violence. Some restrictions apply.

You see, anytime we "adopt" someone or something, we also get the "baggage" from their past experiences. You can't have one without the other. There are always some "strings attached." To his credit, Mack was willing to accept that, and me.

I can't help but sometimes wish my life had been different growing up. I wish I could put the past completely behind me. I wish I didn't have terrible nightmares where I'm trapped back in my parent's home and can't leave. I wish I didn't have to work so hard at opening up to others.

I wish my family hadn't been torn apart when I shared what my dad had been doing to me for years. I know a lot of my family and even friends suspected dad's relationship with me was "inappropriate," but I'm sure they had no idea just how far it had gone. I think, too, they couldn't accept so much evil because that would mean his profession of religion had deceived them.

Every one of us carries our experiences from the past. Old hurts, words said in anger, shame, words left unsaid, hearts broken, divorce, or the loss of loved ones. We all carry something from the past in some form. The trick is learning to let go of what you can and move on – and the right person will help you sort through it. But, you've got to do your part too. You won't ever forget the things that happened to you in the past, but you shouldn't let it taint your life today. If someone hurt you in the past, that doesn't mean you should live the rest of your life expecting everyone else to do the same.

When it comes to doing this successfully and leaving pain from a past experience behind, you must manage your emotions. Managing your emotions doesn't mean burying them or pretending they aren't there. It does mean handling them in such a way that you consider them, consider how they affect you and others around you, and then choose not to let them disrupt the present.

I once heard Liz Murray speak as she told how she went from being homeless and living on the streets and subways to graduating from Harvard. She was living on the streets because she didn't really have a home – her parents were drug addicts. She shared how they didn't have enough to eat because her parents spent all their money on drugs. She shared how they sold all the furniture to buy drugs and how she and her sister would eat ice to feel like they had something to eat.

Liz shared how she ended up living on the streets, and it took her mother dying from AIDS to make her choose to turn her own life around. I can't imagine her life or imagine some of the adversity Liz Murray faced. But, what impressed me is how she shared those experiences, and yet, managed her emotions. You could tell it was difficult. You could tell the memories bring her pain, just like mine do for me, and yet as she shared them, it was clear she has moved on. She lives a full and happy life now as a wife, mother, and motivational speaker.

Regardless of the pain you faced in the past, you have a choice to make. It may be the choice to accept the loss of someone you love. It may be the choice to forgive someone who hurt you. It may be the choice to let your anger or regret go. It may be the choice to let go and let God give you peace. Sometimes wounds break open and only God can stitch them closed.

Today is a gift. Don't waste it by focusing on the things you can't change from the past. Life can only be lived forward.

It's a decision. A choice. And, after you make it, you

will have to manage that decision, maybe every day, maybe forever. Decisions, much like New Year's resolutions, require action to follow through. The decision alone isn't enough – you've got to get up each day and live it.

Today is a Gift – Don't Spend It The Wrong Way

I was at a prayer meeting with a friend and she introduced me to someone there. When that person asked me what I do, I answered briefly (as is my nature to do) "I am a motivational speaker, leadership coach, and author." My friend elaborated, "She is in the full time ministry!"

I started to object. I claim several hats for myself: Christian, Wife, Speaker, Author, Coach, Leadership Trainer, Group Fitness instructor, and so on, but I've never claimed "Minister" as one of them. I've never thought of myself as "Called to the Ministry," and given my conservative early church upbringing where I was taught women should be silent in the church, it almost feels wrong somehow. Please note – I am NOT here to dispute or even comment on religious beliefs about women as ministers. My point here is I would never have said to someone "I'm in the ministry."

There is also a little feeling of unworthiness that contributes to my discomfort with that idea. I can't help but feel God can certainly find someone much better to "minister" to others than me. If God were going to call someone to "minister," He certainly wouldn't call someone like me, with so much sin in the past, to serve.

I've got this ideal woman in my head, and I know I haven't always lived up to the ideal. In fact, I still don't always live up to the ideal. However, I sometimes feel a burden of responsibility – if God has called me for a purpose, then I must honor that, even when I don't want to.

When you consider how God equips us in different ways, it really makes sense that we are ALL in the ministry in some way. We don't have to "be a minister" to be in the ministry. We are all tasked with a purpose to contribute in some way. Indeed, when we are living out our calling and following our purpose, when we are using our gifts, time, talents, and energy to fulfill His purpose, we are "ministering" or contributing.

In "*The Purpose Driven Life*," Rick Warren uses the acrostic "SHAPE" to describe how we are uniquely designed to serve God in different ways: S – Spiritual Gifts; H – Heart; A – Abilities; P – Personality; and E – Experience.

I love this because it points out how each and every one of us are created to serve and to contribute in some way. THAT is our purpose. HOW we do it can be as different and unique as we are because we all have a different "SHAPE."

My SHAPE is different than your SHAPE. In spite of the fact I sometimes feel like my past experiences are the very thing that disqualifies me from helping others, it's actually one of the tools God equipped me with.

I believe meaning and purpose was the missing link in my life five years ago. It wasn't a bad life at all. In 2011, I had a great life, a good job, a decent paycheck, a nice house, a nice car, the occasional vacation, but I wasn't living in my purpose. I didn't have the sense of fulfillment and completion I have today. I didn't have the peace I know today. If God calls me home tonight, I have served well. I don't wake up each morning asking myself, "Is this all there is?"

Discovering your purpose and your "SHAPE" is a process. Each of us live through the process of discovery. However, when you realize the potential of finding and living with passion and purpose, you will value yourself, your time, and your energy much more. You will be much more likely to spend your time well instead of wastefully. Remember, it's your choice, but your choices today will define you tomorrow.

Today is a Gift – Invest In Tomorrow

The problem isn't that there aren't enough opportunities in life. The problem is there are far too many opportunities, and sometimes, we must say no to good opportunities in order to say yes to great opportunities. We either choose to accept where we are in life each day, or we choose to do something about it.

It's not an easy decision to make. I declined three job offers last year, not because they were poor job offers but because they simply weren't in alignment with the direction I'm going. Those opportunities weren't bad, they simply were not great ones for me. So, I gracefully declined.

Learning to say no has been one of the best tools for me to use in appreciating and making the most of the gift of today. Saying "Thanks, but no thanks," means I have complete control over what fills my calendar, and that is an incredible thing in today's crazy busy world. I received an invitation to participate in a Bible study recently, and it sounded like a nice opportunity to study the Bible with some other like minded women – but I'm already participating in one Bible study. More is not always better.

I haven't always been, but I'm now a firm believer in quality over quantity. (This is a good philosophy for dessert too, in case you were wondering.)

It's given me the ability to focus, thus maximizing my time and energy. Because I value my time very highly, I very carefully consider commitments before making decisions.

There are some decisions I have already made, and I don't have to reconsider each time they come up. For example, Mack and I try to spend quality time together on the weekends. I don't have to carefully consider whether to go on a Saturday afternoon hike with him – I've already decided that activity is in alignment with my values. It's part of rest, recreation, renewal, and relationship, all of which are an important part of balance for me.

I do carefully consider anything that happens on Saturday afternoon that isn't in alignment with those things. That doesn't mean I automatically say no, but it does mean I think it through first. I've learned not to immediately answer an invitation, but to request time to consider when I'm not under pressure. This isn't always possible, but when it is, it can be a great way to ensure you are making, and keeping, the right commitments.

Each morning, I ask myself three questions: What will I do today to add value to someone? What will I do today to move forward toward my goals? What will I do today to help me be better tomorrow?

These three questions help me make many decisions about the day because they provide direction and help me stay aligned with my core values.

I must know where I want to go in order to get there. But, once I know where I'm going, it takes self-discipline to ensure I'm making the right decisions to get there.

What am I not doing that I should be doing? What am I doing that I should not be doing? As I look at my day ahead, am I investing in myself and preparing for God's purpose for me tomorrow? My time, talent, and energy already belong to God – am I investing it wisely in His purpose for me?

When I can answer these questions satisfactorily, I know I am living in resilience because I can only thrive when I am living God's purpose for me. Anything less is simply surviving, or Coping.

I want to be able to look back at the end of each and every day and say to myself, "I lived life today Beyond Bound and Broken. I lived life today in Conquest over Captivity, and I lived today well. I lived a life of purpose and passion today. I was a wise steward of what God gave me today."

Can you say the same?

Closing Thoughts

I was in a yoga class one evening, and as we finished up the final resting pose, the instructor walked around and rubbed a little bit of lavender oil on the back of our necks and talked about going into the rest of the week with a mantra or affirmation to repeat to ourselves. She shared two or three, but the one that resonated with me was "I am enough." I think the reason that resonated with me so strong is sometimes I feel like I'm not enough.

What does it mean to be enough? How would I know if I'm enough? How will you know if you are enough?

Simple – we are already enough. Sometimes, we feel

like we haven't found our calling or our passion, and so, we "aren't enough" when we compare ourselves to those that have. Sometimes, we feel like we don't make a big difference in the lives of others, so we aren't enough. It is tempting to look at what we do for a living and think, "It's not important work, and I'm not really making a big difference."

I met a lady at a networking event. When I asked her what she did, she said, "I go around and scoop poop out of people's yards. It's nothing really, just a business I started, and it's nothing important like what you do." The sad thing to me is she really believed SHE wasn't important because the work she was doing wasn't "important." I challenged her because I saw a different perspective. I didn't see someone who "just scoops poop" every day.

When she told me her story, I saw a strong woman who had the courage to step away from a job that required her to work long hours and miss Christmas with her family. She walked away from a job that wasn't in alignment with what she valued – being a mother to her two children and an aunt to her sister's five children. She took a side business that had started as a service – scooping poop – and turned it into a flexible, income-producing service and full time business that enhances the quality of life for her customers and their pets, improves the environment, allows her to enjoy time working outdoors, and also to be available for her most important job – mother to her children and aunt to her nieces and nephews.

When I shared with her how I saw what she does, her whole face lit up. She realized when she changed how she thought about it, it made a difference in how she felt. Same job, same woman, different perspective.

Other times, maybe we have found a "calling" but feel like we aren't equipped to carry it out because it is so much bigger than we are. Sometimes this is my own struggle – am I really enough to carry out this mission God has given me? What happens if someone finds out I'm not perfect? What happens if someone reads my book and realizes I don't have all the answers? Am I enough to be able to help people realize they can make better choices about their life?

It would be so much easier to say, "I can't do it" and relieve myself of the pressure I feel. We are masters at creating excuses in life because we feel like if we cannot do something, then we aren't responsible for failure.

Let me say it clearly – You are enough. I am enough. I am enough to carry out the task God has given me because if I wasn't ready, or if I wasn't "enough," then He wouldn't have given it to me. God challenges us to accept the responsibility for our life, but He does not challenge us beyond what we can handle. I am enough. But, I'm not perfect, and I never will be.

We all face struggles and challenges in life – mine are almost certainly different than yours, and yours are different than someone you know. Overcoming those challenges is what makes us stronger and more prepared for a bigger challenge down the road. Accept the responsibility and acknowledge the fact it won't be easy. You may not always get it right but be willing to learn from your mistakes. Find the peace within that says, "I AM enough."

The perfection of peace doesn't mean everything is perfect – it means you have a sense of inner confidence in who and what you are. Peace doesn't mean we aren't looking to improve, but it does mean we don't beat ourselves up constantly because we feel inferior or inadequate. Peace means, we don't harbor hatred or anger within. It doesn't mean, we don't regret mistakes of the past. It does mean, we learn from them and work to not repeat them.

I won't live my life focused on what could have been. Life is too precious, too short, and filled with too much potential to spend it living with regret for what "could have been, would have been, and should have been."

Find the peace within that comes with making the right choices and standing by them. It's like a battle within, between two people inside you. One wants to be happy, joyful, and peaceful. The other has been beaten or broken to the point of believing all those negative thoughts Satan whispers. Choose carefully which one you will listen to.

Make the choices today and every day that serve you well in who and what you want to be. Choose to be happy. Choose to let go. Choose to smile. Choose your attitude. Choose to forgive. Choose to trust God. Choose to love. Choose to accept responsibility for your emotions, thoughts, and actions. Choose wisely.

Choose Your Future.

God doesn't cause the pain in our lives, but He does use it. Whatever you have gone through in the past or are going through now, never forget God loves you. He has a special purpose and plan for you. If my words have touched your heart, then pay it forward – share a copy of this book with someone else. I would love to hear how this book changed your life. E-mail me at: ria@riastory.com.

The world needs more hope.

Questions for Contemplation or Group Discussion

1. What are your gifts, talents, and abilities? What does your personality enable you to do well? What experiences do you have that God can use?

2. What do you have a heart for and a passion for?

3. What does your personality enable you to do well?

4. What experiences do you have that God can use?

5. Read, reflect and/or discuss these bible verses: Matthew 6:31-34; Acts 20:35; Romans 12:17-21

References & Notes
Chapter One:
1. Robert Morris, *Truly Free Breaking the Snares That So Easily Entangle,* (2015 W Publishing Group, an imprint of Thomas Nelson)
Chapter Two:
1. Sexual Assault Victim Statistics, RAINN, https://rainn.org/get-information/statistics/sexual-assault-victims Retrieved February 29, 2016
2. Viktor E. Frankl, Man's Search for Meaning (1959 Pocket Books, a division of Simon & Schuster
Chapter Four:
1. Jaycee Dugard, *A Stolen life* (2011 Simon & Schuster
2. Reinhold Niebuhr, *The Serenity Prayer*
Chapter Five:
1. Marianne Williamson, *Our Deepest Fear*
2. Joyce Meyer, *Life Beyond Abuse,* (Reprinted via LinkedIn Post entitled "Life Beyond Abuse)
Chapter Six:
1. Janice Pitchford, *Finishing Well: My Daughter's Journey Home* (2015 Janice Pitchford – AAE)
Chapter Seven:
1. Brené Brown, *Daring Greatly,* (2012 Avery an Imprint of Penguin Random House)
2. Bruce Lipton, *Biology of Belief,* (2005 Hay House)
3. James Allen, *As A Man Thinketh,* (Public Domain)
Chapter Nine:
1. Stephen Covey, *The 7 Habits of Highly Effective People* (1989 Free Press, a Division of Simon & Schuster, Inc)
2. Mack Story, *Blue-Collar Leadership: Leading from the Front lines,* (2016 KaizenOps)
Chapter Ten:
1. Rick Warren, *The Purpose Driven Life* (2002 Zondervan)

EXERPT FROM RIA'S STORY FROM ASHES TO BEAUTY

I was 12 when Dad started having some conversations with me about the "facts of life." He would tell me how infidelity in marriage was wrong and so was divorce but "his needs" weren't being met because my mother wasn't able to meet them. I was told they didn't have a physical relationship for many years, but I don't know if that is true. I know she was sleeping on the couch in the living room most nights, she said because of her back. I expect I will never know the truth.

I want to believe she had no idea what was going on, but it's possible she knew and didn't want to face reality, so she shut it out. Either version is hard for me to accept, but there are many things in life we don't want to accept.

I can remember times when Mom was gone, out running errands or something, and my Dad would tell her to take my brother with her. At first, all our talks were about how I needed to be "pure" and stay away from boys until my Dad was able to find the "Right one that God would send." Then, it changed to being all about how a woman was designed by God to meet a man's needs and that was all I was created for. I remember feeling ashamed talking about things like that, but I didn't know what to do. It was the summer when I was 12 when he first started saying how a father-daughter relationship was supposed to be close in every way, physically as well as emotionally. I remember being told I was supposed to give my heart to him "for safekeeping," but I was confused as to why that also meant in a physical way.

One day, my Mom and brother were gone somewhere, Dad and I were sitting in the living room "talking." Somehow, things turned into how wonderful it was that I was the perfect daughter and was so close to my Dad. We went upstairs, and he kept telling me how God intended for daughters to belong to daddies. And, if I would just trust him, he would make sure I lived up to what God wanted. He told me how I was supposed to fill in since my Mother wasn't able to be a wife anymore. He told me I was living up to God's purpose for my life by helping him not have to commit adultery. He told me it wasn't a sin if I helped him like that. He took off my clothes and told me the whole time I was the perfect daughter.

What started out as just taking off my clothes progressed. Within a few months, it wasn't just taking off my shirt and jeans but taking off everything.

Deep in the back of a forgotten drawer, my Mom had hidden a bunch of lingerie she used to wear when she was young, and they were newly married. Dad brought it out one day while we were alone in the house together. He picked out one of the outfits and told me to go in the bathroom. Then, he wanted me to put it on and come out to model it for him. I cried afterward, ashamed of being looked at like that. I was sad for my Mom too – her personal things should not have been shared with anyone, much less her daughter.

Then, the touching started.

ORDER *RIA'S STORY FROM ASHES TO BEAUTY* ONLINE AT: AMAZON.COM OR RIASTORY.COM

ABOUT RIA STORY

Ria is a motivational speaker, author, and professional coach with a passion to help others make the right choices today to reach their goals tomorrow. She triumphed over being sexually abused from age 12 – 19 by her father and escaped by leaving home at 19 without a job, car, or even a high school diploma.

Ria successfully applied leadership principles throughout her career in the healthcare industry, learning to lead at all levels with increasing responsibilities, before resigning from corporate life to pursue her passion for coaching, motivational speaking, and leadership development. Ria holds degrees in Office Administration, Human Resource Management, and a Master's Degree in Business Administration. She is a certified leadership coach, speaker, and trainer with The John Maxwell Team.

Ria is also a fierce health and wellness advocate. She is a certified fitness instructor, teaches group fitness classes several times a week, runs marathons, and is an avid mountain biker – winning the 2011 and 2012 State Mountain Biking Championships in both Alabama and Georgia. She and her husband, Mack Story, live near Atlanta, Georgia.

ABOUT MACK STORY

Mack's story is an amazing journey of personal and professional growth. Mack began his career in manufacturing on the front lines of a machine shop. He grew himself into upper management and found his niche in lean manufacturing and along with it, developed his passion for leadership. He understands that everything rises and falls on influence.

In 2008, he launched, KaizenOps, a Lean Manufacturing and Leadership Development firm offering professional coaching, mentoring, training, and speaking. Mack is a John Maxwell Team Certified Leadership Coach, Trainer, and Speaker. Mack has shared the stage with internationally recognized motivational speaker Les Brown.

Mack is the author of several leadership books: *Defining Influence*, *10 Values of High Impact Leaders* and *Blue-Collar Leadership Leading from the Front Lines*.

Mack is an inspiration for people everywhere as an example of achievement, growth, and personal development. His passion motivates and inspires people all over the world!
Read more about leadership and Mack's personal leadership journey on his website: MackStory.com and BlueCollarLeaders.com

BOOK RIA TO SPEAK AT YOUR NEXT EVENT:

- ➤ Leadership
- ➤ Resilience
- ➤ Ria's Story: From Ashes To Beauty
- ➤ How to A.C.H.I.E.V.E. the Goals in Your Life
- ➤ Dealing with Change
- ➤ Communication & Relationships
- ➤ Time Management/Effective Planning
- ➤ Other keynote topics available on request

Ria also offers Executive Coaching and Leadership Development Training Programs

Call: 334-357-5797
Email: ria@riastory.com
Website & Blog: www.riastory.com

Connect with Ria:
www.linkedin.com/in/riastory
www.facebook.com/Ria.Story.Speaker.Coach.Trainer
www.twitter.com/Ria_Story

Other books by Ria:
Ria's Story From Ashes To Beauty

A.C.H.I.E.V.E – 7 Keys to Unlock Success, Significance and Your Potential

Order Ria's other books online on her website: www.riastory.com

Ria's Story From Ashes To Beauty

Read Ria's inspirational account, in her own words, of growing up as an abuse victim and learning to overcome. Then, learn how she found courage to share her story and find courage for your own. Also available on Amazon.com

A.C.H.I.E.V.E. – 7 Keys to Unlock Success, Significance, and Your Potential

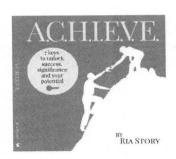

A.C.H.I.E.V.E. is a mini-tip book with short, but powerful, lessons on Attitude, Choices, Humility, Integrity, Energy, Vision, and Excellence.

56926288R00090

Made in the USA
Charleston, SC
03 June 2016